Too many people take too long t
stand their assignment. Landon ~~~ ~ r~~~~~~~~~~ j~~ ~~ ~~r~~~~~g
both in this book. Chapter 3 was the moment for me where I thought,
*"Everyone needs to read this book."*

**RYAN LEAK**
Speaker and author of *Chasing Failure, Unoffendable*, and *The One*
Young Adults Director at Covenant Church—Dallas, Texas

With the pressures we all face today, so many people are left feeling beaten down, disappointed, discouraged and insignificant. What's worse is they often feel as though God views them through eyes of disappointment as well. *Significant* combats this dangerous mindset by illuminating God's truth and offering readers a perspective shift. Landon's passion is tangible, and the message is timely and clear! Read it. Take notes. Live it! And encourage others to do the same.

**ALISON WALLWORK**
Author of *Living Freedom: Losing a Spiritual 10 lbs.*
and *#Momlife Devotional Study*
Campus Pastor of Dream City Church—Phoenix, Arizona

If you are looking for God's purpose and plan for your life, you will want to read this book; you will not be disappointed. Pastor Landon opens up his life in a real and refreshing way to show how God can use anyone and anywhere for His purpose. I was personally encouraged to remember the call of God on my life and my significance in God's eyes.

**LANCE AINSWORTH**
Executive Pastor of Gateway Church—Visalia, California
and Author of *Wilderness Generation*

Landon was called at a very young age to be a kingdom builder. His energy and dedication to growing the kingdom of God and empowering others is contagious. I am proud to be his dad.

**JOSEPH MERRILL**
Dad, and Founding Pastor of Covenant Church—Lake Havasu City, Arizona

# SIGNIFICANT

### DISCOVER • DEFINE • DIRECT YOUR VALUE

## LANDON MERRILL

ISBN: 978-1-951701-21-5 (paperback)
ISBN: 978-1-951701-24-6 (eBook)

Unless otherwise noted, scripture quotations are taken from the New King James Version®. Copyright © 1982 by Thomas Nelson. Used by permission. All rights reserved.

Scripture quotations marked AMPC are taken from the Amplified® Bible (AMPC), Copyright © 1954, 1958, 1962, 1964, 1965, 1987 by The Lockman Foundation Used by permission. www.lockman.org

Scripture quotations marked ESV are taken from the ESV® Bible (The Holy Bible, English Standard Version®), copyright © 2001 by Crossway, a publishing ministry of Good News Publishers. Used by permission. All rights reserved.

Scripture quotations marked GNT are taken from the Good News Translation in Today's English Version—Second Edition Copyright © 1992 by American Bible Society. Used by Permission.

Scripture quotations marked KJV are taken from the King James Version®. Public domain.

Scripture quotations marked NIV are taken from the Holy Bible, New International Version®, NIV®. Copyright © 1973, 1978, 1984, 2011 by Biblica, Inc.™ Used by permission of Zondervan. All rights reserved worldwide. www.zondervan.com. The "NIV" and "New International Version" are trademarks registered in the United States Patent and Trademark Office by Biblica, Inc.™

Scripture quotations marked VOICE are taken from The Voice™. Copyright © 2012 by Ecclesia Bible Society. Used by permission. All rights reserved.

Printed in the United States of America

Produced and Distributed by Breakfast for Seven
2150 E. Continental Blvd., Southlake, TX 76092
breakfastforseven.com

# CONTENTS

# FOREWORD

## ‖

For more than 20 years, I've had a front-row seat to the journey, quest and battle for significance, which Landon describes in this book. Simply reading through his first chapter cast me back into the memories I had with him, beginning in his high school years. As one of the youth pastors at Landon's church and Christian school, I was an eyewitness to his radical transformation. I watched the skinny, little, loud-mouth instigator and troublemaker get kicked out of school and go into a tailspin. I saw the conflicts and verbal attacks he endured and unleashed with those who didn't see his value. I even witnessed another pastor mistreat him and belittle his chances of making it at Bible college or ever amounting to anything in his life. That was shameful. And then I watched Landon prove them all wrong.

I'll never forget the day I saw Landon when he came home for a visit after his first year at Bible college. In nine short months, the skinny, wanna-be-gangster kid had sprouted and matured, as if overnight. He had grown out his hair all West Coast Cali-style and shifted his wardrobe away from "Eminem rapper/basketball thug life" to clean-cut preppy casual. He had a new stride and swagger: his shoulders back, chin high and a look in his eye that confirmed he now saw the world through a different lens.

Landon had left a smart-mouth boy and came home a full-grown man. This was the beginning of our incredible friendship. Now as the head youth pastor at our church, I became a "big bro" of sorts to Landon: a confidant and safe place. I have enjoyed walking alongside him for the last 20 years as he earned the wisdom you are about to read through blood, sweat and tears. Every step of the way, someone was there telling him that he couldn't, that he didn't have what it took, or even to "shoot his dreams in the face." But Landon never quit, never gave up and never stopped dreaming. Now as an adoring husband, doting father and trendsetting local pastor and city leader, Landon drips with the wisdom and experience of accomplishing exactly what others said he never could.

It is with the highest honor that I encourage you to meditate through every single word in this book. Landon is a master storyteller and communicator. The lessons in this book will make you laugh, think and cry. Heck, they might even make you mad at times, as he instigates you to face your fears and sort out the challenges set before you. But this I know for certain, at the end of this book you will understand in a new way, just how *significant* you truly are.

**JOEL SCRIVNER**

Founding Pastor of Oaks Church—McKinney, Texas
Author & Creator of WINology—World Class Performance

# INTRODUCTION

## ||

No matter who we are or what we spend our days doing, we assign value to each aspect of our lives—our possessions, our relationships, our government, our careers ... In our minds, everything has a position of value, great or small. But what about yourself? Where do you stand in that value system? How much do you think *you're* worth? Do you think you're valuable? The answer: You're extremely valuable. You may not realize it, but you *do* have something to offer this world. You *do* have purpose. **You are significant.**

Now, you might be thinking: "Yeah right—I haven't done much to make a difference in life." Or maybe people have actually told you that "you'll never amount to anything" ... or something in between. But the truth is, no circumstance or person—not even you—can set your value. Only God can do (and has done) that! And it's only by the blood of Jesus Christ shed on the cross. He paid that price once and for all. For me and for you. You don't have to allow anything or anyone to try and take that value and change it. God said you are significant, and if that's how He feels about you, then that's how you should feel about yourself.

But how do you change that? Is it even possible?

My life has been tested, challenged, and pressed in so many ways—perhaps like yours. I know what it's like to be overlooked, belittled or just flat out made to feel worthless. But I also know that it's possible to overcome those things and the feelings that come with it. I have constantly had to fight back, come back, and bounce back from all kinds of adversity that tried to destroy who I am and what I am worth. So, I'm not saying it's easy; but it *is* possible. And if I learned to believe that I'm worth a whole lot more than I thought, to stand on that truth and let that guide my life, then anyone can.

On this journey of discovering and defining your significance, you will learn how to direct your value in a healthy way that will always bring a great return. Directing your value towards God, His purpose, and His people will always end up pouring back into your life—instead of being robbed, taken advantage of, or simply just not appreciated when it comes to who you are and what you have to offer.

There's nothing more uplifting in this world than feeling empowered in life, to feel like you are valuable and significant ... and to feel like you've got the right tools to do what it takes.

Part of my calling in life is to help others let go of their past and set (or reset) their true God-given value.

So, will you join me on this journey? Not just on a journey to finishing a good book, but one of faith toward understanding that no matter what has happened to you in the past, you are significant!

# CHAPTER ONE

# A MIRACULOUS BEGINNING

||

I grew up in a Christian home, and my parents were pastors most of my life. On my sixth birthday, one of my presents was church shoes. (Yeah, I know—not very cool or common these days!) And when I say "church shoes," I mean shiny black shoes that were ONLY for wearing to church. Just like basketball shoes are only for the court, these were only for church—just more "holy!" I loved church and dressing up for church, so much my parents knew that I would love this gift. Sure enough, when I opened this gift, I lost it! (The worst *and* best part is that all of this is on video.) When I opened up the box of shoes, I honestly was more excited about them than any other gift. In fact, I shouted out loud, "Neat-o church shoes!" with the biggest smile, followed by me, my brother and my cousin dancing around because we all were so thrilled. Yup, that was "Landon, the little nerdy church kid" who loved dressing up for church.

So it would make sense that the very same year, I knew God had called me to preach. My father had just baptized me, and I came out of the water speaking in tongues. Oh yeah, I was an all-out spirit-filled, water-baptized, church-shoes-lovin' super Christian ... at the ripe old age of 6!

I remember looking at my parents with all seriousness saying, "Mom, Dad—I'm going to be a preacher!" Not surprising since both my father and grandfather were preachers. By the time I was 12, I delivered my first mini-message at an old-time camp revival where my grandfather was preaching. Full disclosure: It was full of "ums" and "uhs"; and I just prayed for someone to save me! Thank God, my grandfather didn't make me sweat it out very long, but bailed me out pretty quickly.

But before that, when I was just nine, I experienced my first miracle from God. I had heard of miracles and healings and even witnessed some in people I knew but never one of my own.

Our hometown of Belgrade, Maine, was a great place in the winter (for kids especially), and there was nothing more fun than spending time with friends flying down a steep, snow-covered driveway on a saucer sled. I was the first kid to sled that day, and I remember the exhilaration I felt as I careened down the driveway. I also remember the moment of panic I experienced when I realized I was headed straight toward a parked car. I don't recall much about the accident, but my neck took the brunt of the impact against the vehicle's bumper, knocking out a piece of my trachea.

As I began to panic and tried to breathe, air could get in but not out. I remember my mother saying my neck had swollen out to the width of my shoulders, and the skin on my chest looked like bubble wrap.

I was rushed to the hospital where the doctors performed a tracheotomy and put some sort of box in the hole in my throat. The surgeon informed my parents it was not likely I'd speak on my own again; he was further concerned about my ability to ever breathe on my own again. My father thanked him for the medical report, and then called for the elders of the church (see James 5:14–15) to come to the hospital.

I was heavily sedated, but awake, when I got settled in my hospital room. Dad and the other men from our church anointed a cloth with oil, laid it on me, and then my dad began to pray. I recall him praying out God's calling on me and declaring the assignment over my life. The men from our church eventually left, and the last thing I remember before going to sleep was my dad at my bedside, praying for me.

When I woke the next morning, the first thing I saw was my dad asleep in the chair. The second thing I saw was the box that had been inserted in my trachea lying in my lap, where it had just fallen as I sat up. The next thing I knew, alarms and buzzers were going off, and the first nurse came in and asked how I was doing and if I could breathe for the first time since the accident. I responded on my own, "Yes, I'm fine." Then the second nurse rushed in, stabbed me with a needle to put me to sleep. (That was *not* neat-o!) They rushed me into the emergency room and cut me "back open." (Yeah, that's right—I was closed up.) They opened me back up only to find that the piece I was missing ... *I was no longer missing!*

Of course, my dad was in awe of what God had done; he and my mom were both in tears, thanking God!

The news about my miracle healing—confirmed by the doctors—traveled quickly around our community. Our local newspaper even published an article titled, "The Miracle Family of Belgrade, Maine." The only evidence of the mishap was the scar on my neck, from where the doctors cut me back open.

Additional childhood accidents throughout my grade school years added more scars to my body. Only a couple years apart from that, I blew off half of my middle finger with a firecracker. For this "wild child," it seemed like every couple of years there was a new accident and scar, my poor parents and more hospital bills. Most of the doctors and nurses knew us by name! The awful side to this is when I went to school with a cast on my hand and kids began to make fun of me, saying, "You're a freak, Landon" or "You gimp!" It seemed to get worse and worse—pretty much becoming part of the norm.

At home Mom always spoke words of affirmation over me. She's what you might call a "smother mother"—always telling me how handsome I was. But even though I never told her what kids said at school, it was like she knew. I guess it's true what they say: Moms always know. They have a sixth sense.

Dad was my steadfast encourager, reminding me who I was and what I'm called to be. Yet, day in and day out at school, I was criticized, ridiculed and mocked by my peers. I wondered, *What does God think of me? Am I worth anything? Am I really a freak?*

The verbal torment continued into my junior high school and high school years as well. But one day, when I was being bullied over the lunch break, a friend came to my defense and pushed the bullies away. As tears streamed down my face, he turned to me and said, "Landon, whatever you do, don't let them see you cry. From now on, you get them before they get you."

That was the instant my life changed.

I went from being victim to instigator—attacking others with my ever-growing vocabulary of trash talking. I wasn't the biggest kid—far from it; and I wasn't the strongest kid either. But I made pushing buttons and tearing down people with my words into an art.

I began to love tearing others down, making them feel small before they had a chance to get to me. My new mantra was "If I hurt you first, I win." For the first time in years, I felt better about myself.

Throughout those years, I only got better at the art of shredding people with my words. In playing sports, I made trash talking and fighting the biggest pieces of my game. In fact, my basketball coach started calling me "Ali" because I was always starting a fight. Unfortunately, it caused me to ride the bench or get sent to the locker room a lot, too. Though God was still part of my life, the emotional pain I'd carried since childhood caused me to run from His call to preach. I was far more interested in playing basketball than going to church, and my wise parents were aware of this. That's why, during my senior year, they offered me two choices for my future: I could go to the college of my choice and play basketball at my own expense; or I could go to Bible college, and they would support me financially.

Well, the decision was easy. I couldn't pay for college, and I was broke; so it was a begrudging "yes" to Bible college—something my high school friends would never have thought possible. My pain drove me so far from God, I went from the eager little "neat-o" church shoes kid to a guy getting kicked out of school, arrested and overdosing the summer before Bible college. So I agreed to go to Bible college; however, in *my* mind, I was only going there to have fun. Imagine my surprise when two weeks into my first semester, I had an encounter with God. He brought back to my mind who I was and what I was called to do—but the thought of being a preacher absolutely terrified me. I remember saying to Him, "I can't do this"; and then He said to me, "Landon, I'm going to be with you."

But who was I to think I could be a preacher? That sounded good when I was an innocent six-year-old; however, moving into adulthood was a different matter. After all, I wasn't exactly the nicest person in the world. At that point in my conversation with God, I was lying face down on the floor, snotting and crying, trying to talk Him out of my being a preacher. But that tactic didn't work. My next move was to try making a deal with God. I said, "I'll do this—only if You show me You are real and are with me every step of the way."

Again He said, "Landon, I will be with you just as I was with Moses, Joshua and every other individual I called according to My purpose" (see Joshua 1:5). With that, I said, "Okay, God, if we're in this, then we're in this." Immediately I felt His peace.

God was indeed true to His promise to be with me throughout my transformation: from a youth who felt like his life was absolutely insignificant into a man who understands the value of his life and calling. The first part of my transformation was in my mind, according to Romans 12:2: *And do not be conformed to this world, but be transformed by the renewing of your mind, that you may prove what is that good and acceptable and perfect will of God.*

I had to renew my mind to what the Word of God said about me. One of my first assignments in Bible college was to memorize 400 verses (perfectly) and be able to write them out. Oh, it felt like a lot! But verse by verse, word by word, my mind began to think, feel and see differently. What God was doing through His word was dismantling the lies of the enemy that had held me captive since childhood: "You are a freak." "Gimp!" "Cry baby." I dismantled those lies by using God's weapons as described in 2 Corinthians 10:4–6: *For the weapons of our warfare are not carnal but mighty in God for pulling down of strongholds, casting down arguments and every high thing that exalts itself against the knowledge of God, bringing every thought into captivity to the obedience of Christ, and being ready to punish all disobedience when your obedience is fulfilled.*

*Change Your Weapon:* First you have to start by realizing that the weapons you once used are no use for this battle. For me it was using "my" words to attack others, hurt others, or belittle others, which were not helping me or useful to making me actually feel better about myself. I had to start using the Word of God to first start speaking better about myself and others.

*Change Your Fight:* Secondly, the fight used to be what others said about me and trying to attack them or defend myself against them. When I started changing who I fought and why

I fought, it reshaped my fight. My fight is against the enemy and strongholds that God has been trying and quite frankly successful at building in my life: to cast down the arguments about who I am and my value as a child of God; to fight against images that don't belong in me and don't shape who I am; to fight against anything that would try to exalt itself above the Word of God over my life.

*Change Your Outcome:* My outcome used to be, "I hate them"; "I hate me"; "I'm not good enough"; "They are worthless," etc. This would only send me spiraling down into negative discussions about myself and about others—only destroying the Word of God and building more strongholds over my life. Now when I changed my weapon and changed my fight, I submitted my mind, my heart, my ways to God. Therefore I changed my outcome. And now, I don't spiral; I submit my thoughts, I don't allow those thoughts and words to run free; I bring them into captivity, submitting them to Christ, destroying the disobedience that would continue to ruin me and allowing my obedience to build me. I had to find ways to submit my thoughts to Christ and to others who believed in me—healthy and God-centered people. My wife is my go-to, along with godly friends and family to make sure I am submitting all things that could lead to disobedient destruction. Bottom line, it's changing the outcome from destroying to building.

Have you ever listened to a lie about who you are? Maybe you're still living by those lies as you read this. But there's good news! You don't have to live that way anymore. You can know the truth and be set free from insecurity, pain, hurt, captivity because Jesus said the truth will make you free (see John 8:31-36). I had to make that decision to stop believing those lies that were said about me and learn to live free.

Once I did that, I had to get control of my tongue. Nothing was going to get better just by thinking good things; it would change by speaking "God things." Good intentions never changed anything; they only come by speaking and doing! Marriages, families, businesses—anything worth succeeding in needs life, truth or love spoken into them! I had to change the way I spoke, and you can too because it makes all the difference.

The Bible says, *Death and life are in the power of the tongue* (Proverbs 18:21, KJV). I certainly hadn't been speaking words of life. The Lord firmly, but gently, led me to the book of James.

> *Even so the tongue is a little member and boasts great things ... But no man can tame tongue. It is an unruly evil, full of deadly poison. With it we bless our God and Father, and with it we curse men, who have been made in the similitude of God. Out of the same mouth proceed blessing and cursing. My brethren, these things ought not to be so.* (JAMES 3:5-10)

Speaking words of life to people seemed foreign to me at first, but I started with baby steps. The first baby step was speaking better about myself. The next (slow) step I began to speak better words—ones that were empowering, encouraging and uplifting, and words that challenged people in a healthy and godly way. Now it didn't happen overnight. It took time, as many people who know me well will definitely attest to. But as I grew in it, I discovered it actually felt good to encourage other people. Next, I moved from speaking words of encouragement to speaking words of faith to those around me. The words I chose to speak comforted people, healed them and blessed their souls. I heard my heavenly Father say, "Landon, this is what you are made for."

And as I learned to bless others with my words, I was also blessed by the words of pastors and ministry leaders who came alongside me, saying, "Landon, God is using you in a powerful way." "Landon, we see the Spirit of God moving in your life." "Landon, you are making a difference in the lives of others." As I poured into others' lives, God sent people to pour into my life! Sometimes the enemy, as well as our own minds, will try and deceive us into thinking that if we pour everything into others, we won't have anything left. But, let me tell you, that is the complete opposite of the truth! The more you work with God and pour out to others, the more He fills you up!

Now God had a plan for my life before I was born, and I discovered that plan at an early age. But the enemy also had a plan, which Jesus identified when He said, *"The thief does not come except to steal, kill, and to destroy. I have come that they may have life, and that they may have it more abundantly"* (John 10:10). The devil first tried to kill me, but he couldn't. So, he then did everything he could to keep me from my calling. He convinced me there was something wrong with me—that my life was worthless, without significance, not important or valuable in any way!

I've since learned that the devil uses this tactic on many believers, and that I'm not the only one who feels this way. You may have not had a severe accident or people bullying you in school; but maybe you had an abusive parent, a destructive loss or a terrible tragedy in your life. The details may be a little different, but the tools of the enemy are the same! Those tools are demonic tactics to keep you cloaked with doubt, unbelief and shame—unable and unwilling to step out in faith and fulfill God's plans for your life. But here's the good news of the Bible: *For this purpose the Son of God was manifested, that He might destroy the works of the devil* (1 John 3:8, KJV).

Jesus destroyed the works of the devil in my life, and He will do the same for you. In the rest of this book, I invite you to join me on a journey of faith to understand that no matter what has happened to you in the past, you are significant! You can experience this significance and live this life out knowing how significant you are, living life to the fullest as Jesus promised in John 10:10.

## SIGNIFICANT APPLICATION

1. What are some promises from God you need to start speaking over yourself?

   _____

   _____

   _____

   _____

2. What miracles or blessings have you said no to because you don't feel worthy or valuable enough for God to really do it for you?

   _____

   _____

   _____

   _____

3. Is there a moment in your life where something happened to you that caused you to question your value? If so, how? And were you able to come through that challenge?

   _____

   _____

   _____

   _____

# CHAPTER TWO

# *NOTHING IS BY CHANCE*

||

The word *significant* is defined as "important and deserving of attention; of consequence; of **great value**." There's not a person on Earth who is not significant, of great value in God's eyes. The problem is, we oftentimes fail to see our own significance because we view ourselves through the lens of the world and its standards. Especially with what the entire world faced in 2020. According to Chris Hodges in *Out of the Cave*, we have seen suicide hotlines spike 900%. One out of four thought of suicide in this nation, and the children's hospitals in our state of Arizona were being filled up with children who were trying to take their own lives! Statistics say that this generation deals with more anxiety and stress than soldiers who fought in World War II! My heart cries out for every single person to know how valuable they are.

As I think about this matter of my own significance, the Lord first took me to two Bible passages: one in the Old Testament and one in the New Testament to help begin painting a picture of applying truth to our lives by establishing our value. The first was a story about Jesus, described in the book of Luke:

> Now it happened, the day after, that He went into a city called Nain; and many of His disciples went with Him, and a large crowd. And when He came near the gate of the city, behold, a dead man was being carried out, the only son of his mother; and she was a widow. And a large crowd from the city was with her. When the Lord saw her, He had compassion on her and said to her, "Do not weep." Then he came and touched the open coffin, and those who carried him stood still. And He said, "Young man, I say to you, arise." So he who was dead sat up and began to speak. And He presented him to his mother.
>
> Then fear came upon all, and they glorified God, saying, "A great prophet has risen up among us"; and, "God has visited His people." And this report about Him went throughout all Judea and all the surrounding region. (LUKE 7:11-17)

I want to call attention to two points about this story. First, the effect this miracle had on the people. They were all filled with awe as they recognized a great prophet had appeared among them. Second, the woman in this account was never named.

The Lord then led me to the book of 2 Kings and the story of another woman who also went unnamed.

*Now it happened one day that Elisha went to Shunem, where there was a notable woman, and she persuaded him to eat some food. So it was, as often as he passed by, he would turn in there to eat some food. And she said to her husband, "Look now, I know that this is a holy man of God, who passes by us regularly. Please, let us make a small upper room on the wall; and let us put a bed for him there, and a table and a chair and a lampstand; so it will be, whenever he comes to us, he can turn in there." And it happened one day that he came there, and he turned in to the upper room to lay down there. Then he said to Gehazi his servant, "Call this Shunammite woman." When [Gehazi] had called her, she stood before him. And [Elisha] said to him, "Say now to her, 'Look you have been concerned for us with all this care. What can I do for you? Do you want me to speak on your behalf to the king or the commander of the army?* (2 KINGS 4:8-13)

Have you ever wondered, *Do I matter? Does anyone even know my name? Am I making a difference with my life?* God's answer to these questions is a resounding *yes!* Your life *is* of great value, it is changing history and matters so much beyond all you can imagine. Whether or not others know your name, God does!

At the end of v. 13, the Shunammite woman gave an interesting answer to Elisha's question: *She answered, "I dwell among my own people."* In a more modern vernacular the phrase "I dwell among my own people" could be rendered as "I'm fine." Have you ever had someone say that ... "I'm fine"? It's usually in response to "How are you?" ... Or, "Do you need anything?" The typical and expected response is usually, "Oh, I'm fine." Oftentimes, it's a greeting at church: "Hello, it's great to see you; how are you doing?" ... "Oh, I'm fine." But truthfully, we are far from "fine."

The Bible describes the Shunammite as a notable woman—clearly a woman of means; she was able to provide food and private housing for the man of God. She had no material needs, yet there *was* something she lacked ... "She was not fine" as Elisha learned when he questioned his servant, Gehazi.

> *So he said, "What then is to be done for her?"*
> *And Gehazi answered, "Actually, she has no son, and her husband is old."*
> *So he said, "Call her." And when he called her, she stood in the doorway. Then he said, "About this time next year you shall embrace a son."*
> *And she said, "No, my lord. Man of God, do not lie to your maidservant!"*
> *But the woman conceived, and bore a son when the appointed time had come, of which Elisha had told her.*
> (2 KINGS 4:14–17)

I continued to read the story of the woman and her son, wondering why God had led me to this passage. But then I began to see the initial and obvious connection between the two Bible stories found in the books of Luke and 2 Kings: both women had lost their sons. When the Shunammite woman's son had grown to the point he could work in the fields with his father, he one day fell ill and died. She wasted no time in calling for Elisha, who came immediately (see 2 Kings 4:32–35).

Elisha was a prophet of God, and Jesus not only holds the office of prophet but also priest and king. Though their lives on Earth were separated by more than 800 years, certain similarities marked the miracles performed by the two men—one of which was that both raised a woman's son from the dead.

Elisha first spoke to the Shunammite woman's heart and then gave her a son, whom he later raised from the dead. Centuries later, when Jesus stepped into His earthly ministry, He did the same thing in the city of Nain, restoring the widow's son to her. In fact, they almost take place at the same location. There are so many similarities and connections between the two stories.

You may ask, "Why are these stories important?" Because they demonstrate a key principle: When God moves in the lives of people, nothing that happens is ever by chance. You are not alive on Earth at this precise time by accident. You are not reading this book at this exact moment by chance; rather, God has a specific word for you, and He is calling you into His perfect timing.

Think about this: Jesus didn't just *happen* to be walking through the city of Nain and all of a sudden say to Himself, *Oh, there's a funeral going on. I didn't know this was going to happen.* No! Jesus knew where He was to be—the perfect moment to show up at the exact location where God could demonstrate His love and power for all to see.

In fact, in the story in Luke, Jesus and His disciples were with a large crowd leaving the celebration of the centurion's servant who was healed. (I will talk more about that in a later chapter.) But here is this celebration running into a funeral procession—one crowd is happy and rejoicing full of faith and hope; the other is mourning and in sorrow.

Let me ask you a question: What happens to you when God's joy meets your sorrow? For this woman, she had lost everything, and her world was literally ending right before her eyes! But the procession of joy, hope and faith couldn't have come at a more perfect time! I'm sure she was like many of us—at her wit's end and ready to quit. But Jesus shows up right on time! Oh yeah, God has his perfect timing for everything!

Not only was it right on time for her, but it was right on time to fulfill the purpose of God in the earth ...

Jesus said, *"Most assuredly, I say to you, the Son can do nothing of Himself, but what He sees the Father do; for whatever He does, the Son also does in like manner"* (John 5:19). Jesus being God in the flesh—the Word made flesh—had already seen and known His Father work through the prophet Elisha to raise the Shunammite woman's son; and in like manner, He raised the widow's son in His day.

The miracle Jesus performed that day was only natural for Him, yet it was significant for the woman, her son and all who witnessed. In essence, Jesus is saying to us, "What comes natural to me will be significant for you." Or, what's supernatural for us is just natural for Him. It's easy and second nature for Him. I love that we serve a supernatural God who looks for ways to do a significant work in our lives and wants to show you that you are not forgotten. Your life is significant, and you are of great value.

I can imagine what the widow in Nain might have been thinking the day of her son's funeral: *First I lost my husband, and now I've lost my son. Where is God? Do I even matter anymore?* But then Jesus showed up—not only for the woman but also for her son. The young man was raised from the dead, and the woman got her son back.

An important takeaway here is that Jesus touched the very thing that represents limitations and the end for this boy and his mother. He touched the very thing that said, "It's all over—this is as far as you go." Jesus will always start by touching the area of your life where you were told, "It's over, this is as far as you can go, you'll never amount to anything, you'll never make it, you'll never be good enough, you'll never be better, go farther, do more ..." He will always start by touching that area first because He will cause you to jump right out of it—surpass it, overcome it, go beyond it! As you take this journey of stepping into your significance, be prepared to jump right out of that coffin, right out of those limitations that were put on you! And realize that it's not the end; it's just the beginning.

## SIGNIFICANT APPLICATION
||||||||||||||||||||||||||||||||||||||||||||||||||||||||||||||||||||||||||||||||||||||||||||||||||||||||||||||||||||||||||

1. What areas in your life do you need to let God touch so that He can take off the limitations?

_____

_____

_____

_____

2. Make a list of things in your life that have been determining your worth and value. (e.g., career, education, possessions, status in your community)

_____

_____

_____

_____

3. Have you ever had a moment of sorrow or disappointment but God brought you an opportunity for joy and encouragement? If so, how did God do that?

_____

_____

_____

_____

CHAPTER THREE

# *LESSONS FROM THE SHUNAMMITE*

‖

As we delve deeper into the Old Testament story of the Shunammite woman, we find two particular biblical truths pertaining to our value, both of which are relevant in our day and time.

1. *Our individual value does not come from our wealth, nor do our achievements define the anointing over our lives.* In other words, our worth does not come from our wealth but from the One who established us on this earth.

In the *Amplified Bible* of 2 Kings 4:8, it says, *One day Elisha went on to Shunem, where a rich and influential woman lives* (AMPC). Similarly, other versions of the Bible describe her as prominent, a woman of influence, important and wealthy. Although this prominent woman of Shunem had notable wealth and wielded great influence, neither of these attributes defined her significance regarding what Elisha did for her in returning her son from the dead. Her value was not determined by her wealth, her achievements or her social pedigree.

Likewise, our value in God's kingdom is not determined by our bank accounts, achievements or social status. We make a mistake when we base our value on the amount of money we have or the positions we hold in life; to do so is like taking a roller coaster ride that never ends. The ride might be fun for a while, but it would be an exhausting place to live on a continual basis.

You may say, "But aren't we God's workmanship, created to do good works?" (see Ephesians 2:10). Yes; however, our value is not determined by our works. Even when we are at our worst, when we do absolutely nothing, we are still valuable in God's eyes. When we've totally messed up our lives and don't accomplish a single thing for God, He still sees us as valuable. Remember this: We are human *beings* not human *doings*, made in the very image of God. You are valuable and significant by just **being you!**

So, it doesn't matter if you live in a gated country club community or on the proverbial "other side of the tracks." It doesn't matter if you have a college degree or a GED, if you can trace your family heritage for generations or don't know who your parents are. (None of us come *from* our parents; we come *through* them.) None of these things define our value. Our value is established by the One who created us, who knew us while we were yet in the womb. Jesus said, *"Are not five sparrows sold for two copper coins? And not one of them is forgotten before God. But the very hairs of your head are all numbered. Do not fear therefore; you are of more value than many sparrows*

(Luke 12:6). God loved and values us so much that He gave us His only Son.

We need to continually live in the knowledge that God loves us and has established upon each of us an intrinsic value that we may not completely understand. God loves us more than we can comprehend or ever know, so let's stop bringing our resumes to God; instead let's bring Him our hearts!

2. *Our value is not based on how others treat us.* It's interesting to note from the story of the Shunammite that when Elisha and his servant entered the room built for them, Elisha didn't speak directly to the woman who'd been so generous to him. *Then he said to Gehazi his servant, "Call this Shunammite woman." When he called her, she stood before him. And then [Elisha] said to him, "Say now to her, 'Look you have been concerned for us with all this care. What can I do for you? Do you want me to speak on your behalf to the king or to the commander of the army?'"* (2 KINGS 4:12-13)

We don't know for certain why Elisha initially didn't communicate with the woman—because when she returned to the room later in the story, Elisha and the woman spoke directly to each other as he prophesied that she would have a son. But we can imagine how she might have felt. She'd essentially just built him a private apartment on her estate to use without charge anytime he wanted, yet he didn't even acknowledge her after he'd requested her to come to him. The woman could easily have been offended and felt devalued because of the way the man of God treated her, but she apparently did not.

I personally believe Elisha was challenging his benefactor so that he could determine where her heart was. She had wealth, prominence and influence; but more importantly, she had a heart for God. She didn't allow her perception of the way the prophet treated her determine her value.

Oftentimes we allow the way others treat us establish our value. We may ask ourselves, "Have I been praised enough today?" or say, "What I really need right now is a good pat on the back." Living our lives in accordance with the praise—or the criticism—we receive from others is never productive nor satisfying. What others say about us does not determine our value. Our value comes from God, who established His Word in us because He loves us.

I am always pleased when people compliment my preaching or my messages. I think it's foolish and really a touch of false humility when we act like we don't want ANY kind of encouragement; but it is just as foolish and dangerous to chase after or dwell on it.

One Easter Sunday, a first-time visitor to our church approached me after the service and said, "When you began to speak this morning, I had to ask myself, 'Did Joel Osteen just take the stage?'"

Of course, I was blessed that in his opinion I was in the same category as one of the world's best-known preachers.

I always appreciate kind words; however, I have learned the hard way to not allow them to determine my value. I've learned that if I choose to live off the praise, then I can easily die from the criticism.

As a pastor I must be especially aware that my value is not established by how others treat me or what they say to me.

I remember when I was 24 years old, my father asked me to preach in his absence at his church in Lake Havasu City, Arizona. My message was about dreaming and imagination; and after preaching my heart out, I said to myself, *Wow—that was awesome!*

But as I left the building with a box of materials in my arms, a man walked up to me and said, "Man, I couldn't follow you. You were sporadic, erratic and all over the page. I can't wait until your dad gets back!" He ranted on for a few more minutes as I stood there holding the box, telling me over and over that I was crazy—that I wasn't good enough for him. Afterward I felt absolutely destroyed. I felt as if I'd failed my dad, and when I got to my vehicle, I sent him a text message saying how terrible I'd done and never wanted to preach again. I was ready to give up. But when my father responded with a phone call, he said, "Landon, what you said isn't true," and then he began to speak life into me.

Two weeks later, a photo of the man who'd severely destroyed me in the church parking lot appeared on the front page of the local newspaper along with a story telling of his arrest. It had been determined that he was unstable and was admitted to a mental institution.

I've since come to understand that those who are our harshest critics oftentimes do what counselors refer to as "projecting." This means they say to others the things they really feel about themselves. So now, when someone says to me, "Your preaching isn't deep enough" or "You don't teach enough doctrine," ... or "That was the worst preaching ever" (and yes I've heard these), I don't let their comments stay with me. Now again, I get tested in this area every once and a while, and I have to remind myself of the same truth and principle: My value comes from His Word not their opinion. And your value and worth should also come from His Word. Each time you get tested—and you will be tested repeatedly—just go back to the truth.

When we stand on His truth, we don't need any direction other than from the Holy Spirit, for God has called His children out of the darkness—away from the words of the enemy—and into His wonderful light (see 1 Peter 2:9).

Ask yourself: *Have I allowed the way other people treat me determine my value?* If so, I challenge you to make the decision *right now* that you are no longer going to live this way. Your value does not come from the way others treat you nor what they may say to you or about you. It doesn't matter how many times you may have failed or how much you've messed up your life. God loves you despite your past poor choices and bad decisions. All you need to do is turn to Him and say, "Father, I'm nothing without You." Reflect on what Jesus said about your Father: *"If you then, being evil, know how to give good gifts to your children, how much more will your Father who is in heaven give good things to those who ask Him!"* (Matthew 7:11).

## MAKE ROOM FOR GOD

I've read the account of Elisha and the Shunammite woman many times since the Lord first directed me to it. I contemplated my own significance, and that of every other man and woman created by God. In addition to seeing the practical truths that can positively impact our lives, I now also see another powerful piece to this message within the story.

Elisha was recognized as a man of God—a prophet. Simply put, Elisha was a man who carried the Word of God. He passed by the Shunammite woman's home regularly and often stopped in for food. But then something happened; the woman decided to add on a room designed specifically for Elisha's personal use.

What she did was, of course, of practical assistance to the prophet; however, in essence she had just made room in her life for God. She had previously experienced contact with the Word of God that Elisha carried on a regular basis, but then, all of a sudden, she decided, "I can't live with only a little bit of God. I need to invite Him into my home, to be a part of my life." I see her decision as an Old Testament type and shadow of the body of Christ that was to come in the New Testament. Those very first Jewish believers in Jesus the Messiah no longer gathered in their synagogues; rather, they met in their homes.

But what about us today? What does it look like to make room for God? Just like the Shunammite built a room and then added a lamp and a table to create the perfect space for the prophet of God, our making room for God begins with our making *time* for God—time spent in prayer and reading His Word. I want to challenge you to ask yourself these questions: Do I want God in my home today? Do I want Him in my life? Do I want Him in my business? If the answer to these questions is *yes*, then start making room for Him in your schedule.

Most people's problems lie right here in making room in their schedules and their lives. Because when it comes down to it, they just want Him there occasionally when it's convenient. Many of us don't want to interrupt our busyness—our games, practices, school, work, vacations or personal time. We want God to make us feel better without costing us anything. If we say things like, "I can't afford to tithe," or "I'm not going to give that much money," what our hearts are really saying is that we want more out of God and from God than we are willing to invest!

But when you make room for God, He always makes room for you. Spending time with God and appreciating His value in your life is the first step in understanding your own value.

When we make time for God, we literally increase our capacity to receive from Him. Many believers are quick to say they want more of God, but they've never taken steps to increase their capacity to receive what He has for them. Not spending time with God yet asking for more of Him would be like pouring fifteen ounces of water into an eight-ounce glass. That glass is incapable of receiving all that is being poured into it. I once prayed this way, but then God said, "If you'll make more room for Me, I'll pour out more. But you first have to make more room for Me in your life. You've got to adjust your schedule so that you spend more time with Me and in My Word."

Once I did as God instructed, my capacity to receive increased, and I was able to experience more of what He wanted to pour into me.

It's really important to remember that when we receive Jesus Christ as Lord and Savior, we have everything that dwells in Him: *For in Him dwells all the fullness of the Godhead bodily; and you are complete in Him, who is the head of all principality and power* (Colossians 2:9–10). We already have the fullness of the Godhead dwelling in us; however, we *can* increase our capacity to receive all that has been prepared for us. This includes health, prosperity, favor, blessings, wisdom, revelation—and the list goes on.

I recently read a business book that beautifully illustrated the point of increasing our capacity to receive. The book talked about IQ (intelligence quotient) and EQ (emotional quotient), both of which are measures of an individual's intelligence and emotional capacity. But the thing that caught my attention was what the book described as our AQ, meaning our ability to adapt or adjust to change. As human beings, we have this God-given ability.

When we decide to make room for what God wants to do in our lives, we are able to adapt and adjust so we can receive all He has for us. In turn, God says, "Thanks for making room. Now, what can I do for you? How can I help you, and what can I give you today?"

God has something great for each and every one of us, but receiving what God has for us begins with our decision to make room for Him. When we do, He always shows up and asks, "What do you want? What do you need in your finances, in your family?" When this happens, let's not reply as the Shunammite woman did, saying, "Oh, I'm fine." Jesus taught

His disciples about prayer and spoke of the importance of *asking* God for those things they needed or desired.

> *"So I say to you, ask, and it will be given to you; seek, and you will find; knock, and it will be opened to you. For everyone who asks receives, and he who seeks finds, and to him who knocks it will be opened. If a son asks for bread from any father among you, will he give him a stone? Or if he asks for a fish, will he give him a serpent instead of a fish? Or if he asks for an egg, will he offer him a scorpion? If you then, being evil, know how to give good gifts to your children, how much more will your heavenly Father give the Holy Spirit to those who ask Him!"*
> (LUKE 11:9–13)

Most of us are familiar with the King James version of James 4:2, which says, *Ye have not, because ye ask not*, but let's look at two other translations of this powerful truth: *You do not have what you want because you do not ask God for it* (GNT); and *You do not have because you have chosen not to ask* (VOICE). Clearly, God puts the responsibility to *ask* Him for what we need squarely on our shoulders. According to God's Word, we are to be bold in our asking: *Let us therefore come boldly to the throne of grace, that we may obtain mercy and find grace to help in time of need* (Hebrews 4:16). The apostle Paul said, *Be anxious for nothing, but in everything by prayer and supplication, with thanksgiving, let your requests be made known to God* (Philippians 4:6).

I want to encourage you that if you have a need in your life, find another believer in your church or circle to agree with you in prayer. However, as a pastor, I would be remiss if I didn't give you this word of wisdom: *Be ready to fight!* When the Shunammite woman's son died, she didn't first run to her husband to tell him the news—she went directly to Elisha.

Why would she not go to her husband? Because *she* was the one who'd fought the battle to believe she would conceive, and it was now up to her to fight the battle to *keep* the miracle God had given her. In essence she was saying to God, "You promised me a child and then You gave me a son. You did as You promised, and now You must protect what You've given me; You must uphold what You blessed me with." The Shunammite woman stood firm on the promise of God, and as a result of her faith, she received her son back from the dead.

It's ok to fight for the favor God has given you—to know that difficulties come with destiny, and burdens come with blessings. Ask any parent: Every child is a wonderful blessing, but that doesn't mean there's not a burden. But the good part is, you can overcome the difficulty, and God will give you the grace to carry that burden!

I pray that what I've shared within the pages of this book so far has gone into your heart and is now stirring your soul. Don't allow yourself to remain comfortable with any area of barrenness in your life, and don't allow any physical, emotional or spiritual pain related to that barrenness to remain. Allow God's promises to come alive and be confident that the Holy Spirit will speak to you. Perhaps you've incorrectly believed your value comes from a source other than God, or that others are of more valuable because of their accomplishments. If that's you, then simply repent and declare out loud, "God, my value comes only from You!" And now pray this prayer:

*Lord, I thank You for every truth You've revealed and every word I have received. I will not allow pride to stand between me and a move of the Holy Spirit in my life, and I refuse to yield to any insecurity and fear that may oppose my receiving all that You have for me. I will not allow what others say about me define my value, which comes only from You.*

*I choose today to make room for You, knowing that as I do, You will make room for me. I choose to conceive new life today, for You are faithful to perform Your Word. I am willing to fight for Your promise because I know You will uphold and protect every blessing that is mine in Christ Jesus, in whose name I pray. Amen.*

## SIGNIFICANT APPLICATION

1. What areas have you been saying, "I'm fine," but you are really not fine?

_____

_____

_____

_____


2. What words from people, good or bad, have shaped who you are?

_____

_____

_____

_____


3. Out of those words, which ones are not of God and need to be let go?

_____

_____

_____

_____

# CHAPTER FOUR

# THE PRICE IS RIGHT

||

When I was a Bible college student, I had a friend named Billy. He was a wonderful young man who loved God and always gave Him thanks, even for the smallest of blessings. Billy would say things such as, "I just want to thank God that my shoes are comfortable"; "I had a headache and now it's gone—praise You, Jesus"; or "Thank You, Lord, for this beautiful day." He was the kind of guy who just wanted to thank God for everything, big and small.

I remember when Billy decided that a Palm Pilot (a handheld device before smartphones) would help him with his studies and keep track of his schedule. He began to research the different brands and prices and discovered the cost was more than he could pay at the time. But in true "Billy fashion," he said, "You know what? I'll pray about it, and I'll wait. In the meantime, I'm thankful for my old phone."

A short time later Billy decided he could make a little money by selling his car and putting the money toward a new car, specifically a Mercury Cougar. But he had two problems:

One, he couldn't sell his car for the price he wanted. Two, he didn't have enough credit or money in his bank account to secure a loan. As expected, Billy said, "Oh well, I'm thankful for my old car and will continue to pray about a new one."

While Billy was on a business trip to Los Angeles, he decided for his day off he wanted to go do something fun while he was there. How about going with a few friends to *The Price Is Right* to see if they can get on the show? He got in line, got in the audience, and was one of the first people to hear that classic "Come on down!" call to contestants' row!

But the story gets better.

"The first item up for bid" was—wait for it—a Palm Pilot! Billy knew the exact price of the device and won that round. He took the stage next to Bob Barker as the announcer named the next item available if the price was right: a brand-new Mercury Cougar. Not only did Billy win the Palm Pilot and the Cougar, but he won the whole showcase. Crazy, right? He won everything because he knew the right price.

The point I want to make is this: Once the price of something has been set by its maker, there can be no negotiation. There can be no haggling over its value, which is determined solely by its creator. This life isn't a garage sale, yard sale or pawn shop! Your value isn't negotiable; your significance isn't bargained for.

Likewise, you and I have a set value. The Word of God says, *For you were bought at a price; therefore glorify God in your body and your spirit, which are God's* (1 Corinthians 6:20). Your value was established over 2,000 years ago when God paid the price for you through the death of His Son, Jesus Christ. You were bought and paid for before you were even born, before anything, good or bad, happened in your life. Your value was set before you knew your name. It's as if God said, "I came to set the standard, to establish the value of My dear child." Jesus paid the price; therefore, there can be no haggling over your value—by either you or others. And the price He paid was right! You could say He paid the highest price and became our High Priest. You see, the moment you made Jesus your Savior and Lord, He also became your High Priest.

> *Seeing then that we have a great High Priest who has passed through the heavens, Jesus the Son of God, let us hold fast our confession. For we do not have a High Priest who cannot sympathize with our weaknesses, but was in all points tempted as we are, yet without sin. Let us therefore come boldly to the throne of grace, that we may obtain mercy and find grace to help in time of need.*
> (HEBREWS 4:14-16)

Knowing that Jesus, our High Priest, intercedes continually on our behalf assures us that when we have a need, we can approach God with boldness and confidence (see Romans 8:34). No matter the need, whether large or small, we should always take those needs to the Lord instead of trying to meet them ourselves.

The book of Hebrews has much to say about the power of the ministry of Jesus Christ, particularly as it pertains to the New Covenant God established by Jesus' atoning death, burial and resurrection:

- *And inasmuch as He was not made priest without an oath (for they have become priests without an oath, but He with an oath by Him who said to Him: "The LORD has sworn and will not relent, 'You are a priest forever ...'" by so much more Jesus has become a surety of a better covenant.* (HEBREWS 7:20-22)

- *But now He has obtained a more excellent ministry, inasmuch as He is also mediator of a better covenant, which was established on better promises.* (HEBREWS 8:6)

- *To Jesus the mediator of the new covenant, and to the blood of sprinkling that speaks better things ...* (HEBREWS 12:24)

In other words, we can say Jesus came to make everything that pertains to life *better* for those who receive Him as Savior and Lord. He said, "*... I have come that they may have life, and that they may have it more abundantly*" (John 10:10). Then, as He spoke to Mary following His resurrection, Jesus said, "*... but go to My brethren and say to them, 'I am ascending to My Father and your Father, and to My God and your God'*" (John 20:17). With those words, Jesus proclaimed that a touchable, tangible, Father-child relationship with God Almighty was within reach for all who desired it.

But not all desired such a relationship. In the book of Mark, we find a conversation Jesus had with the Pharisees, the religious leaders of the day. They believed in, and strictly adhered to, the traditions handed down from their religious predecessors, and they expected the same of everyone else.

> *Then the Pharisees and some of the scribes came together to Him, having come from Jerusalem.*
> *Then the Pharisees and scribes asked Him, "Why do Your disciples not walk according to the tradition of the elders, but eat bread with unwashed hands?"*
> *He answered and said to them, "Well did Isaiah prophesy of you hypocrites, as it is written: 'This people honors Me with their lips, but their heart is far from Me. And in vain they worship Me, teaching as doctrines the commandments of men.' For laying aside the commandment of God, you hold the tradition of men— the washing of pitchers and cups, and many other such things you do."*
> *He said to them, "All too well you reject the command- ment of God, that you may keep your tradition ... making the word of God of no effect through your tradition which you have handed down. And many such things you do."*
> (MARK 7:1, 5–9, 13)

Jesus revealed that the tradition of man makes the Word of God of no effect. We can plainly see that whereas religious tradition creates distance between God and mankind, Jesus brought reconciliation and relationship. Throughout His earthly ministry Jesus proclaimed, "Behold! The kingdom of heaven is at hand. It's within your grasp. You can touch it." He was preparing His followers for the soon-to-come time when they would no longer meet with God in a synagogue or temple made with man's hands; rather, God would dwell *within* them because Jesus came to establish a better covenant, to make life better.

## *TRUTH VS. TRADITION*

Most of us are familiar with the Bible story about Jesus healing the woman with the issue of blood. Let's see what happened when truth met tradition that day.

As Jesus headed to the house of a young dying girl, the Bible says He was thronged (crowded) by a multitude of people. The story of the woman unfolds ...

> *Now a woman, having a flow of blood for twelve*
> *years, who had spent all her livelihood on physicians*
> *and could not be healed by any, came from behind and*
> *touched the border of His garment. And immediately her*
> *flow of blood stopped.*
>
> *And Jesus said, "Who touched Me?"*
>
> *When all denied it, Peter and those with him said,*
> *"Master, the multitudes throng and press You, and You*
> *say," 'Who touched Me?'"*
>
> *But Jesus said, "Somebody touched Me, for I*
> *perceived power going out from Me." Now when the*
> *woman saw that she was not hidden, she came trembling;*
> *and falling down before Him, she declared to Him in the*
> *presence of all the people the reason she had touched Him*
> *and how she was healed immediately.*

*And He said to her, "Daughter, be of good cheer; your
faith has made you well. Go in peace."* (LUKE 8:43-48)

Once again, we are not privy to the name of the woman in
such an important story of Bible history. It amazes me how
many unnamed people in the Bible have impacted lives for
centuries! Life can feel like that sometimes—when you're not
rich, famous or the most popular. Life can feel like we don't
matter but again, this woman who will remain nameless will
also remain with us forever! When Jesus asked who touched
Him, she came trembling with fear—and she had good reason
to be afraid. According to the religious Jews, it was inappro-
priate for a woman to touch a man, even her husband, in
public. What's more, Jewish law deemed her ritually unclean
due to her condition and required her to remain secluded. The
fact that she went out in public could have resulted in severe
consequences.

But notice how Jesus—an itinerate Jewish rabbi—dealt
with her. Instead of reprimanding her, He addressed her as
"daughter" and then said, "Be of good cheer; your faith has
made you well. Go in peace." In the midst of a multitude,
Jesus commended her faith for all to see and hear. Religious
tradition said, "She is an unclean woman. Let her remain at
home. It's not a woman's place to be here around the men."
Religious tradition said she was of less value than a man; it
tried to distance her from God; it tried to control her. But then
Jesus—the Truth—came along and faced tradition head-on.
And the multitudes watched as Truth demolished tradition that day. Throughout your life, always remember this

wonderful lesson: When you feel like God is only going to be angry or be upset with you because you didn't do something right, you messed up or weren't perfect, remember Jesus turned to that woman and said "daughter." Now knowing that we will have a daughter, that's all my mind can seem to go to; I picture my daughter coming to me with an issue or upset or hurting. What kind of dad would I be if I corrected her before I helped her?!? A terrible one, that's what! Jesus turned to the woman as only a father could and spoke love, healing and acceptance over her! With one touch and one sentence, He changed her life! Remember that when God turns to you, it's not to chastise you but to help change you with one touch and one word!

As believers, we too must be aware of religious tradition and how it can affect our lives. It's easy to take a verse of scripture and turn it to our own truth. Doing this is dangerous, for it diminishes the truth of what God really wants to do in our lives. Any time we study a Bible story or a scripture, we need to ask ourselves three questions: Who is speaking? Who are they speaking to? And, importantly, what did they know that we don't know? Jesus, a Jew, most often interacted with other Jews, for He said, *"I was not sent except to the lost sheep of the house of Israel"* (Matthew 15:24). The culture and traditions of their day were very different from ours, which is why we must not make the mistake of interpreting biblical truths with modern Western-world standards.

For instance, the apostle Paul penned these words to the church in Corinth: *"Let your women keep silent in the churches: for it is not permitted unto them to speak ..."* (1 Corinthians 14:34,

KJV). If we try to interpret this verse based on our culture, some 2,000 years after the Bible was written, it might appear that Paul said women are not allowed to speak in church. Period. Sadly, there are some who have taken this verse, twisted it entirely out of context, and created a false doctrine literally prohibiting women from speaking in church.

When in fact, the Jewish synagogues had separate seating sections for men and women—a custom likely carried over into the fledgling church. If a woman wanted to ask her husband a question during the service, she had to speak loudly enough for him to hear, obviously disturbing others in attendance. Paul went on to say in verse 35: "... *let them ask their husbands at home ...*" which makes perfect sense considering the custom of their day.

This and other incorrectly misinterpreted scriptures pertaining to women have hurt members of the body of Christ. Some leaders have said, "Oh, we'll let women lead worship, but they'll never preach to men!" Jesus didn't pay a greater price for a man and a lesser price for a woman—He paid one price for all. Women can preach just as well as men can!

Jesus did not distinguish people based on gender, race, culture, social status or any other traits that characterize and separate us as human beings; rather, He came to break down those walls.

Paul said it this way: "*For you are all sons of God through faith in Christ Jesus. For as many of you as were baptized into Christ have put on Christ. There is neither Jew nor Greek, there is neither slave nor free, there is neither male nor female; for you are all one in*

*Christ Jesus. And if you are Christ's, then you are Abraham's seed, and heirs according to the promise"* (Galatians 3:26–29).

Paul also said, *"For all the promises of God in Him are Yes, and in Him Amen, to the glory of God through us"* (2 Corinthians 1:20). In other words, we are all equal in the eyes of God: We've *all* fallen short of His glory. But the good news is that Jesus paid the price for our redemption once and for all, and now *all* of God's promises belong to *all* believers—with no strings attached.

## RADICAL FAITH

As we continue to study the story in Luke 8 of the woman with an issue of blood, we see her desperate desire to be healed from a condition that had gone on for 12 long years.

When facing a problem or situation that has gone on longer than we think it should, it's easy to fixate on the matter. As we dwell on the situation, it becomes the biggest issue in our lives—bigger even than our identity in Christ—and we soon lose sight of our value. The danger in this scenario is that when our problem dominates our thoughts and conversations, in essence we are praising the problem. Praise and worship are what I give my attention, effort, time and thoughts to. And the biggest problem with that is when I praise my problem, my problem gets bigger; I magnify my problem. But God wants us to praise Him because that magnifies Him in our lives!

When we magnify our problem, it's no wonder that we can neither see God nor find a way out of the darkness of that problem. As a result, our problem seems bigger than our God. This is a major issue for everyone, especially when trying to establish value and significance on this earth, because if our problem is big and our creator is small, then that makes us terrified; we feel like we can't do anything! And when we feel powerless, we feel hopeless.

David, who faced Goliath looked at his giant and wasn't scared at all unlike the rest of the army, because David could see beyond his problem into his promise! David said, "... *I come against you in the name of the* LORD ..." (1 Samuel 17:45, NIV). In other words, his God was bigger than his problem. He turned to the only source of true power that could help him and all of Israel.

## SHUT THE DOOR

When Jesus arrived at Jairus' house, the only people He allowed inside with Him were the girl's parents and Peter, James and John—the three disciples who had accompanied Him. He purposefully ordered everyone else to leave. Why would Jesus do such a thing, literally shutting the door in the face of those who wept and mourned? Because they were filled with fear, doubt and unbelief. When He told the mourners everything would be okay, they mocked and ridiculed Him; therefore, Jesus allowed only five people to surround Him. I want you to write down this principle, get it in your heart, say it out loud, memorize it and make it part of your daily declaration: SHUT THE DOOR! Yep, it's real simple and real short, but every time you say it, you need to remember what it means. It means that when you need faith in your life, shut the door on doubt—on the naysayers. When you need something positive in your life, shut the door on negativity. Be less concerned with the feelings of those around us or with what's happening in the world and more concerned about the faith inside of us or what we allow into our home.

The picture looks like this: If a boat is out on the sea, it will always be fine as long as the sea stays outside the boat. If not, that's when the sinking begins. Don't let what's surrounding you get in you, because that's when it becomes dangerous to your life! People you work with or go to school with may talk negatively or tell dirty jokes; but you can shut the door and surround yourself with those of faith, filling you heart, mind, soul and your home with hope and peace!

Now the pastor in me and the voice of my wife in my head are both telling me to make sure there is balance. Just because you shut the door on those things doesn't mean you burn the bridge or totally cut people out of your life. Jesus simply just shut them out of the house; they were still outside and still somewhat a part of their life—just with some healthy boundaries and healthy distance.

## NEW FRIENDS

When you surround yourself with people of faith, they will help elevate your faith and cause it to grow. Picturing growth, I want you to think about this phrase "what you tolerate you cultivate." In other words, what you allow to be closest to you will be what grows in your life. Make sure you are cultivating and growing the right things in your life. When it comes to getting the right things around you, know that it (or they) will make you and your whole life better. There are lots of trees and plants that when planted around or near each other their roots will grow deep in the ground searching for the others to connect to—not to hurt or harm the other but to strengthen and help each other. The trees that do this become so connected and strong that it becomes 100 times harder to uproot because they are connected to a healthy system that support them.

Now weeds and tares are the opposite; they take, harm and hurt everything around them. They steal the nutrients, water, and sometimes even sunlight from the healthy plants only to end up destroying them both.

If you find yourself surrounded by doubters, you need to find new friends. Pull out all skepticism, disbelief, discouragement and doubt. You don't have time for it, so shut the door. Doing so is your decision, but the Holy Spirit will help you. Jesus paid the price for you, and your life is too valuable to allow your destiny to be determined by doubt and unbelief (see 1 Corinthians 15:33).

## A SIMPLE WORD

A couple years ago, I was called to the hospital to pray with someone's family member who was a patient there. Of course I said yes even though I knew very little about the situation. When I arrived at the hospital, I was greeted by the people who attended our church, letting me know that their uncle had tried to take his life. Using a gun, he had blown the back right side of his head open but survived! His young teenage daughter found him and called 911 right away. He was now at the hospital and unresponsive, surrounded by about 15–18 family members. My church members began to tell me that some of the family in the room don't believe in God and hate church!

Now as a pastor I played it cool, smiled and nodded. But inside I was thinking, *What am I doing here?* I began praying to myself in the spirit! I was angry, a little nervous, but I asked the Holy Spirit what to say and do, expecting Him to tell me ... "The Lord says in the third hour of the seventh day he shall rise and awaken by the power of God almighty!" and maybe a light would shine down so that all could see the glory of God. But that didn't happen, and He didn't say that. He did say, "Speak hope and love." Let me tell you: When I heard that, I was actually upset! What kind of soft, cookie-cutter, easy word is that? These people are going to push me right out of the room!

Nonetheless, when we arrived, I walked into a full room, was introduced to one person at a time. Everyone was of course somber, crying and disheartened. I simply said, "My name is Landon, I'm their pastor, we are here for you all, we love you, and we are praying for you." I continued to let them know that if they needed a place to stay, a meal or anything at all, to not hesitate to ask. As I worked my way around the room, I stopped at the daughter—she was of course just overwhelmed and distraught by it all. I began to tell her the second part of the word: "There is hope." When I said that, the whole room got quiet and was listening (it kind of shocked me). I told them there is hope because we could be in a different room, planning different things; but we are here, and he is still alive. I asked if we could pray, and we all joined hands, surrounding the bed and I said a simple, short and sincere prayer.

I honestly don't even remember what I said, but then at the end like all prayers I said, "And we all say ... amen!"

At those words, the man sat up from his bed for the first time and spoke!! He began to ask for water. The nurse on duty stood up in tears and went to get someone and some water. The whole family was in shock and awe, crying in amazement! I simply said, "Who believes in God now?!" Then and there they all gave their lives to Jesus! After we were walking out of the room, the family began to tell me why speaking hope made such a big difference. They said right before I came, the whole family was talking about how if there was just a sign of hope, then they would know everything would be ok—that they all just needed a little bit of hope in a dark moment where there seemed to be none! I was blown away and suddenly the word the Holy Spirit gave me made sense. (I repented to the Lord for my attitude at first hearing it.)

## WHAT ARE YOU FEEDING?

Returning to the story of Jairus, imagine the level of faith in the room when his daughter opened her eyes and rose from the bed. With my mind's eye, I see those gathered in the room crying with excitement and simultaneously laughing, elated with hope and joy again. The parents look at their baby girl standing with Jesus, His arm around her as He smiles at them. They filled their room with the right people, and Jesus had a word of life and hope to give ... and it changed everything.

But that's not quite the end of the story, for the Bible goes on to say, ... *And [Jesus] commanded that she be given something to eat* (Luke 8:55).

51

How interesting.

I'd read other Bible accounts of Jesus raising people from the dead, but He'd never instructed anyone to feed them. So, I asked the Holy Spirit, "Why did Jesus do that? Why did He command that she be fed? Is dying really that exhausting?"

I'll never forget the Holy Spirit's response: "You don't feed the dead; you only feed the living." *mic drop by the Holy Spirit!* Let me ask you a question, "What are you feeding?" While you think about that, let me tell you this simple truth that hit me right between the eyes; and the more I pondered it, the more the Holy Spirit revealed. When we come to Jesus and ask Him to be our Lord and Savior, we may say something like this: "Lord, I give You my life. I'm dying to the old me and asking You to create a new me. The same resurrection power alive in You is now alive in me. I've got new hope, a new life and new desires." We declare one life has died and a new life has begun.

However, oftentimes the sad part is we continue to feed the "dead life" and not the new one. We still feed the desire to party, we still fuel our envy and jealousy, and we keep pouring into our insecurities and pride. This is why we get so frustrated, thinking, *I gave my life to Jesus, and things haven't gotten better. I surrendered to Him as Lord of my life, and I still don't see any growth, improvement, health or security.* Then we turn our concerns to frustration, then anger, bitterness and resentment towards God, church, pastors, leaders—blaming others for what we neglect to do and fail to see. That frustration may also sound like this: *My church doesn't have enough small groups; my pastors and leaders don't communicate; our women's ministry doesn't do enough; God never speaks to me ...*

It's easy to lose sight of what's really important because we are feeding on all the wrong things—including media, socials, news, etc. And it doesn't take long for frustration to set in.

The Bible says, *"Therefore, if anyone is in Christ, he is a new creation; old things have passed away; behold, all things have become new"* (2 Corinthians 5:17). This is, of course, true; yet our flesh wants to go back to the way it used to operate, and we end up trying to feed the old dead habits and our old lifeless self. That's why the Word of God tells us, *And do not be conformed to this world, but be transformed by the renewing of your mind, that you may prove what is that good and acceptable and perfect will of God* (Romans 12:2).

There is an old adage that says, "If the Word of God really was your daily bread, would you be starving or full?"

Just as our physical bodies require natural food to live and flourish, so our spirits require spiritual food to live and flourish. And that spiritual food is the Word of God. Feeding daily on the Word of God enables us to finally walk away from our old, dead lives and step into the purposeful, passion-filled life God has planned for each of us.

You may say, "That's fine for you and others, Landon, but you don't understand how much pain I've suffered in my life—spiritual, emotional and physical." While that may be true, there's good news: God knows everything about you. His desire is to heal every aspect of your being. And it doesn't take Him long to finish the work in you (see Philippians 1:6).

Perhaps you need Him to heal your marriage and make it new, or free you from a disease. Maybe you need to be delivered from that addiction and have your mind restored. Don't make the mistake of listening to the lies of religious tradition that say, "Well, maybe it's the Lord's will that you just have to suffer for Jesus." No! Jesus suffered for you, He died for you, and it is *His will* to heal and deliver you! All you need to do is make the decision to be radical in your faith, reach out to Him just as the woman with the issue of blood did, and receive your miracle. Decide today to begin feeding and fueling the new you, and let the old you fade far into the past and die.

Through His Son, Jesus Christ, God has already paid the price for you, and your value has been forever established. I invite you to pray this prayer:

> *Lord, thank You for showing me how valuable I am, how worthy I am. I receive Your worthiness and righteousness, and I receive my healing and deliverance. I refuse to live in discouragement and doubt a moment longer, for they are from the enemy.*
>
> *I speak to the spirit of fear and command it to leave me and my family, for Your perfect love casts out fear. I choose faith over fear, and I receive all that You have for me.*
>
> *I will not let my pain become my identity, rather I now give my pain to You that through it You may manifest Your power and reveal Your purpose for my life. I thank You that all Your promises are yes and amen, and they are mine in the powerful name of Jesus. Amen.*

## SIGNIFICANT APPLICATION

1. What are some things you can be thankful for today?

_____

_____

_____

_____

2. How can you start to feed the right things in your life?

_____

_____

_____

_____

3. Who are your current top five people in your life?
   And should they continue to be?

_____

_____

_____

_____

4. Who are some more faith-filled people you can bring
   into your life?

_____

_____

_____

_____

**5.** *What are some bold steps you can take to live your best life?*

_____

_____

_____

_____


**6.** *List 3 ways you can help remind yourself of your value.*

_____

_____

_____

_____

# CHAPTER FIVE

# YOU HAVE A GOD-GIVEN ASSIGNMENT

||

By now, you should know that you are not reading this book by chance, whether someone gave it to you or you purchased it yourself. God knew you would be reading this book at this precise time, discovering just how unique and significant you are and the vital role you play in fulfilling His plan for your life in our world.

The prophet Jeremiah, who lived some 600 years before the birth of Jesus, described the moment he learned of God's plan for his life: *"Then the word of the LORD came to me, saying: 'Before I formed you in the womb I knew you; before you were born I sanctified you; I ordained you a prophet to the nations.' Then said I: 'Ah, Lord God! Behold, I cannot speak, for I am a youth.' But the LORD said to me: 'Do not say, "I am a youth ...," 'for I am with you to deliver you,' says the LORD"* (Jeremiah 1:4–8).

You may say, "Well, I'm certainly not called to be a prophet to the nations, so what does that passage of scripture have to do with me?" My point is this: The words God spoke to

Jeremiah are just as applicable for you today and for your God-given assignment.

Notice Jeremiah didn't feel qualified for what God had called him to do (I know how that feels), but God's response was "I am with you." Perhaps you know your assignment from God, or maybe you have yet to discover it. The difference between Jeremiah's day and our day is that as New Testament believers, each of us have both a *calling* and an *assignment*. We share the same *calling*, often referred to as The Great Commission, spoken forth by Jesus in Mark 16:15–18: "... *Go into all the world and preach the gospel to every creature ....*" Though our *calling* is the same, our *assignments* differ. My assignment is to carry out my calling as a pastor of the local church. Others are assigned to carry out their calling in the workplace, at home, in volunteer service to others, or in any of a thousand other positions and places throughout the world where people need to hear the Gospel.

Wherever and whatever that may be, remember God is with us wherever we go. He is with me right now, as I write these words, and He is with you right now as you read them. God is moving in your life at this very moment—and a change is about to take place. This is both an exciting place to be and a difficult one as well.

Why? Because the devil knows you've got a heavenly assignment, and he's got an assignment, too. He's going to do everything he can to see to it that you don't fulfill what God has called you to do, where He's called you to be, and who He has called you to be with. And there are three main ways the enemy will try to stop you:

1. Sending discouragement
2. Bringing a distraction
3. Making a deal

But Jesus said, *"Behold, I give you the authority to trample on serpents and scorpions, and over all the power of the enemy, and nothing shall by any means hurt you"* (Luke 10:19). Jesus has given us authority over all—not some—but *all* the power of the enemy. The Lord demonstrated what this authority looks like when He encountered two demon-possessed men.

> *When He had come to the other side, to the country of the Gergesenes, there met Him two demon-possessed men, coming out of the tombs, exceedingly fierce, so that no one could pass that way. And suddenly they cried out, saying, "What have we to do with You, Jesus, You Son of God? Have You come here to torment us before the time?"*
>
> *Now a good way off from them there was a herd of many swine feeding. So the demons begged Him, saying "If You cast us out, permit us to go away into the herd of swine."*
>
> *And He said to them, "Go." So when they had come out, they went into the herd of swine. And suddenly the whole herd of swine ran violently down the steep place into the sea, and perished in the water.* (MATTHEW 8:28-32)

Jesus also exercises His authority in a very well-known story of Him and the disciples in a boat on a stormy night.

Jesus looks out the window of the home they are staying in Galilee across the sea and more than just seeing the natural He sees something more. But all He says is, "Let us cross over to the other side."

The disciples, after seeing Jesus teach for a while welcomed a little break and some traveling, so they set sail. Along the way, Jesus fell asleep, a storm came, and the disciples got scared. As the ship came under the power of the storm and they all felt everything was in jeopardy, they woke Jesus in a panic. Now the interesting thing is they said, "Master, master, we are perishing!" They didn't wake Him up and say, "Jesus, what should we do?" Neither did they say, "Jesus, we know You have the power to heal, deliver and save ... tell us what to do with this storm." They didn't come to Him with any kind of hope of knowing that He's the one who said "Let's cross over"—that it was His mission. They did not come to Him with any kind of faith or courage; they came to Him in a panic, completely discouraged.

This is what all of us will face at different points in our lives: a storm of discouragement. Now Jesus wakes up, silences the storm and hushes the waves. Then He turns to His disciples and says, *"Where is your faith?"* The disciples turn to each other and say, *"Who is this that even the winds and waves obey Him?"* (see Luke 8:22–25).

Let's pause and talk about the first way the enemy is going to try and stop you from walking in your assignment and living the significant life He called and created you for.

## SENDING DISCOURAGEMENT

Storms of discouragement are something we can all relate to. Your storm might look like the crushing weight of debt and the darkness of bankruptcy looming over you. It might be a storm in your marriage, a difficult situation with your children, or an attack of cancer in your body. Maybe you are in school, and the storms of anxiety and the pressure of the wrong culture are pressing all around you. It could be internal struggles like depression, thoughts of suicide and loneliness causing you to feel discouraged and disheartened. But these storms are the very things that can actually become indicators to encourage you. Because when the storm is sent to stop you, it means you are getting close to breakthrough—you are on the right track. All you need to do is rise up in faith, belief and hope, knowing that He who called you will also carry you! He will never let you down, never leave you or forsake you; and He has empowered you to do what He did: silence that storm of discouragement! This storm that was sent to cause fear should now start causing faith to arise! For He has not given us the spirit of fear but of power, love and a sound mind (see 2 Timothy 1:7). Don't let the storm stop you. Keep moving forward because you are too important for discouragement to detain you and too valuable for it to destroy you.

## BRINGING A DISTRACTION

The journey continues, and Jesus and the disciples press on to Gadarenes, opposite of Galilee. When Jesus stepped out of the boat, a man who had been demon-possessed came running (see Luke 8:26–39). Now this man was naked, had been cutting himself, couldn't be restrained, had dwelt in tombs, was filthy, and did I mention ... naked?! And running to Jesus! Now, if that's not distracting, I don't know what is. What we see here in Scripture is that Jesus gets out of the boat, but we don't really know about the disciples getting out nor do we even hear from them again during the whole interaction!

Remember, these guys are the ones who were going to be empowered to build the church and change the world; and right when they arrive at the place that Jesus said to go, they are suddenly out of the equation.

But we can't get too mad at the disciples, whether they got out of the boat or stayed in it because this is what happens to a lot of us. Right when Jesus gets us through some of the biggest storms in our lives—delivering us from bankruptcy, healing us of cancer, restoring our marriage, or bringing fresh joy and peace in our life—we somehow check out and get distracted by what's around us and who's suddenly been brought into our world.

I've seen it happen too many times: People pray, "God, deliver me," "God, if you'll get me out of this, I swear I'll ..." and God comes through and delivers them. But then all of a sudden, it's like they aren't even there. They check out, they get distracted or just busy with their own stuff. We see Jesus deliver them from the storm only for them to get distracted or even possibly intimidated by the demon-possessed man; and this is where the enemy works his second tool on us. If he can't stop us from getting to where God calls us and who God calls us to, then he will bring a distraction in our life.

The art of distraction is a skill used by every magician, manipulator and even some politicians. The enemy is going to use anything he can to distract you even when you are in the right place with the right people. You could even be in church—right place, right people—and still be thinking about lunch, not even engaged with the worship or message. Or you're probably thinking about the craziness happening at work, having wild thoughts of drama with friends, or even dwelling on offenses and hurt feelings.

I've seen God bless people's finances only for them to suddenly be too busy for church, and somehow unable to tithe. I've watched God restore families and marriages only for them to get distracted and not have time for God and His house but have plenty of time for sporting events and vacations.

Now I know this may sound harsh, but God will never be able to bless your agenda while you neglect His assignment! Even being too busy with something beneficial to your body like healthy eating and fitness can be distractions. Don't get me wrong: I believe we should all eat healthy and work out. But if you are spending more time on building your body than building the body of Christ, you may need to refocus and redirect your attention. Don't let the enemy win with the tool of distraction. Set your focus on Christ, and be determined like the prophet Isaiah, setting your face like flint to the Lord (see Isaiah 50:7). The opposite of distraction is focus, and the tools you need for focus are right in front of you: the Word, worship, prayer, fellowship, giving, serving and accountability. I call these "the magnificent 7" because with these, you'll always win!

Continuing with the story in Luke, Jesus then looked at this demon-possessed man and asked him his name; the demon answered, "Legion" (see Luke 8:30). Now *legion* not only means "many," but it is also a militant word. What I want you to remember is this: While the enemy deals in chaos, it does not mean he doesn't have a strategy. The enemy has a plan and a strategy for your life. This isn't meant to intimidate you; it should only remind you that when things happen, it did not happen by chance. Have you ever said, "That came out of nowhere" or "I didn't see that coming"? It's usually not attached with something positive. I'm here to tell you that those things—those distractions and attacks—are not random.

These demonic spirits have been around for a long time, and they have been coming after you long before you knew. The same tricks that they played on your parents, grand-parents, and great-grandparents, they are trying to play on you. These are familiar spirits, but we don't need to take too deep of a dive here because we don't want to give them credit because they don't deserve any. All it calls for is a simple mention for attention. That drug addiction wasn't random; it was strategic. That marital issue wasn't random; it was strategic. Oppositional things that come running at you in life are not random but strategic. Now take heart because the strategy of the enemy fails and falls at the feet of Jesus! Your significance is greater than any scheme the enemy plots against you.

After the demons responded, Jesus told them to go and be cast out. So now they begin to try, beg, plead with Jesus to be sent into the pigs that were there on the hillside. Shortly after they do, the pigs run off the hillside into the lake and drown.

(see Luke 8:31–33). This shows that they wouldn't have been permitted to stay in that area no matter what they had wanted.

## MAKING A DEAL

Since the enemy couldn't stop them with a storm—which we know was not by chance—and that the enemy couldn't distract Jesus from His assignment, the enemy decided to try and make a deal with Him. This is what the enemy will do with us every time we try to walk in our assignment and significance. If he can't beat us, then he'll try to deal with us. I've seen the enemy try to make a deal with people, saying, "You can go to church with your family on Sunday, even Wednesday, but I'll keep the other days." In other words, live like hell on Friday and Saturday, then try to get to heaven on Sunday.

Or he'll try to convince people to only talk about Jesus at church but don't speak about Him at work. Maybe it's a deal that you'll worship at church but not at home; pray around other Christians but not around strangers; go to church but never give; surrender your heart but not your thoughts; give Christ your eternity but not your day-to-day.

It's that all-too-common notion of giving every area of our lives over to Christ except that "one area!" Whatever it is, the enemy is going to try and negotiate a deal through that one exception because he's intimidated by you. But stand your ground. Don't let your flesh keep control; don't let the enemy keep a place, and don't give a foothold because it will infect every area of your life. The enemy is in the place of weakness and insecurity, so don't take any deal he has to offer because it's always less than what you can take (see Ephesians 6:10–18).

## THE TERRITORY

Now you don't want to miss the whole point of this story! After the man as delivered from the demons, the whole town came out and couldn't believe what happened. The man wanted to go with Jesus, but Jesus told him to go and tell the story (see Luke 8:37–40). Gadarenes was the gateway of 10 provinces, and it was on the other side of Galilee. So first off, he became a witness to his whole town and a soon-to-be witness to the whole area. Then think about it: Galilee was a Jewish region, but in Gadarenes, there were farmers raising pigs. You may or may not know this, but pigs were unclean (not kosher) for the Jews—not permissible to eat or touch; so what Jew would be raising pigs …? Answer: none. So when Jesus says, "Let's cross over to the other side," I think it meant more about supernatural transformation and less about geographical transition. It wasn't random; it was a significant move for a significant assignment.

Because right after He delivered that demon-possessed man, He gets back in the boat and goes back to the other side! That means He went to heal one unknown man and impact an area full of Gentiles! Right there is a good place to get excited because that means Jesus will cross though whatever He has to just get to you! Jesus was showing us that He was there for the Gentile and the Jew long before anyone knew! Now we know that Jesus already did that for us by going to the cross, coming out of the grave, and taking the keys of death, hell and the grave for us. "Death, where is your sting? Grave, where is your victory?" (see 1 Corinthians 15:55).

This was all about a significant assignment of taking territory. Your personal value will always be attached to your personal assignment, and your assignment will always be connected to a territory.

## GOD-GIVEN ASSIGNMENTS

My assigned territory is currently Flagstaff, Arizona, and surrounding areas as the Lord directs. God has graced us and anointed my wife Emily and me to minister here with power and authority! We have seen demons cast out, as well as been on the receiving end of amazing generosity. Before moving to Flagstaff, I had been a campus pastor of a mega church in Dallas. There came a point after six years of trying to build a satellite campus here in Flagstaff, that the church leadership felt it would be better for us to move back to Dallas and work at the main campus. Now we knew we were called to Flagstaff (and Arizona); God had given us a heart for this area, but as they were trying to bring us back to Dallas, they were also saying that *they* didn't have a vision for this area, which meant they were about to close up shop, and we would be without.

We began to pray, "Lord, lead us and guide us; and if You are calling us to be here, we need You to provide!" I asked some leaders to come together and pray for a building and direction on September 16, 2017; and the very next day I had a meeting with a police chaplain. We met for coffee so he could share his testimony, and he told me how he was a pastor with a small (debt-free) church congregation, and that he was battling cancer. He continued to tell me how he had watched me work with the police department, prisons and outreach around town and felt the anointing of God on me. He also told me that he didn't know what to do with his building and that he just wanted it to continue being used for the glory of God.

Now to tell you the truth, I wanted to jump across the table, grab ahold of him and tell him exactly what to do and that is to give me the building! But I played it cool and smooth by the grace of the Holy Spirit and said, "Well, let's go pray over it, and the Lord will reveal." So we went and prayed, and after a while of praying, he came over to me in tears and said, "I know this sounds crazy, but I feel like God is telling me to give you this building!"

I began to tell him my side and what all was happening. We wept, laughed and praised God! God had gone before me, and even when I could have been discouraged, distracted or made a deal that would have compromised my assignment, I remained steadfast; and God provided to help us take the territory!! Now we have a debt-free building with multiple services packed out, and God is causing us to thrive—right in the territory He called us to take!

Jesus has already done the "heavy lifting" where our God-given assignments are concerned. All we need to do is obey God, saying, "Okay, Father, I'm going to get in alignment with Your assignment. I'm going to agree with You and step into that new calling, new dimension, and new place where You've assigned me." Jesus has made a different way of living available for us—if we're willing to release the pain of the past—for He said, *"The thief does not come except to steal, and to kill, and to destroy. I have come that they may have life, and that they may have it more abundantly"* (John 10:10).

I love the way Jesus enters our lives and then shows us a different way of living—an abundant way of living. But I also know how difficult it can be to embrace this good news, especially when we've been wounded through pain. In the book of John, we find the story of an encounter between Jesus and a woman who'd experienced painful wounds in her life.

> *Therefore, when the Lord knew that the Pharisees had heard that Jesus made and baptized more disciples than John (though Jesus Himself did not baptize, but His disciples), He left Judea and departed again to Galilee. But He needed to go through Samaria.*
>
> *So He came to a city of Samaria which is called Sychar, near the plot of ground that Jacob gave to his son Joseph. Now Jacob's well was there. Jesus therefore, being wearied from His journey, sat thus by the well. It was about the sixth hour.*
>
> *A woman of Samaria came to draw water. Jesus said to her, "Give Me a drink." For His disciples had gone away into the city to buy food.*
>
> *Then the woman of Samaria said to Him, "How is it that You, being a Jew, ask a drink from me, a Samaritan woman?" For Jews have no dealings with Samaritans.*
>
> *Jesus answered and said to her, "If you knew the gift of God, and who it is who says to you, Give Me a drink, you would have asked Him, and He would have given you living water."*

*The woman said to Him, "Sir, You have nothing to draw with, and the well is deep. Where then do You get that living water? Are You greater than our father Jacob, who gave us the well, and drank from it himself, as well as his sons and livestock?"*

*Jesus answered and said to her, "Whoever drinks this water will thirst again, but whoever drinks of the water that I shall give him will never thirst. But the water that I shall give him will become in him a fountain of water springing up into everlasting life."*

*The woman said to Him, "Sir, give me this water, that I may not thirst, nor come here to draw."*

(JOHN 4:1-15)

Jesus had yet another God-given assignment that day, for in the first paragraph of the story above it says, "But He needed to go through Samaria." Jesus' assignment wasn't just geographically necessary; He had a significant assignment to go visit that woman. When He got to His destination, Jesus sat down at the well, dusted Himself off, and appeared not to know who else would show up that day. I envision Him being all chill and relaxed as He waited for His assignment to arrive for her divinely appointed moment of transformation.

Notice Jesus had sent the disciples into the city to buy food (see verse 8). He didn't need their help as He intervened in the life of the woman who was about to step into her God-given assignment. Jesus initiated the conversation by asking for a drink of water. This was not an unnatural request; however, the woman recognized He was a Jew. As I've mentioned

before, when reading a story in the Bible, we need to understand who was speaking, to whom they were speaking, and
what they knew that we might not know. In this instance, we
need to understand there was a long-standing hatred between
Jews and Samaritans, which went back to the days of the patri-
archs and the time when Jacob's brothers tried to do away
with him.

When the woman pointed out the obvious to Jesus—Jews
had no dealings with Samaritans—Jesus took the level of the
conversation from the natural to the spiritual, speaking of
a fountain, or well—of *living water*. The woman had no idea
where to find that well, yet she asked Jesus to give her that
water. That's when He again redirected the conversation.

> *"Jesus said to her, 'Go, call your husband, and
> come here."*
> *The woman answered and said, "I have no husband."*
> *Jesus said to her, "You have well said, I have no
> husband, for you have had five husbands, and the one
> whom you now have is not your husband; in that you
> spoke truly."*
> *The woman said to Him, "Sir, I perceive that You
> are a prophet. Our fathers worshipped on this mountain,
> and you Jews say that in Jerusalem is the place where one
> ought to worship."*
> *Jesus said to her, "Woman, believe Me, the hour is
> coming when you will neither on this mountain, nor in
> Jerusalem, worship the Father. You worship what you
> do not know; we know what we worship, for salvation*

*is of the Jews. But the hour is coming, and now is, when the true worshipers will worship the Father in spirit and truth; for the Father is seeking such to worship Him. God is Spirit, and those who worship Him must worship in spirit and truth."* (JOHN 4:16-24)

## THE RIGHT WAY TO WORSHIP

Jesus' discussion with the Samaritan woman about worship is noteworthy for us as the body of Christ. I often see people who essentially rob themselves of a move of God in their lives in favor of their religious preferences. For instance, they may go to hear a Christian speaker or attend a different church with a friend. Because the pastor's preaching style and the worship are different than what they are accustomed to, instead of entering into God's presence, they essentially stiff-arm the move of the Holy Spirit. Religious preference becomes prejudice when left undealt with. Prejudice looks like deciding the pastor is too young or too old, the music is too fast or too slow, or that the people don't dress the way they "should" in church.

We must take care that we are never callous in the presence of God when it comes to worship. One of the things Jesus did when He showed up at the well was pull down the wall of separation in worship. In essence He said, "It's not about who is right or wrong, about how you worship or where you worship. Those who worship God worship Him in spirit and truth." Jesus' words are just as true for us today as they were when He first spoke them to the woman at the well in Samaria. If you know you have prejudices, it's time to let them go. If you're not sure, then ask the Holy Spirit to reveal anything that needs to be addressed—to bring it into the light and make it known. Then make the steps to challenge yourself, get healing and freedom.

## REVEALING AND HEALING WOUNDS

Jesus already knew everything about this woman: the pain she'd experienced and the wounds she'd suffered. He strategically directed His conversation with her to bring these issues to light so that she could be healed. Judging by the passive-aggressive shots she took at Jesus regarding His being a Jew and her having no husband, His words had certainly hit the mark.

Perhaps you too have experienced pain in your life—we all have. Maybe you are critical because you were criticized during your growing-up years. Or you're negative because during those years someone always spoke pessimism over your hopes and dreams. Now, as an adult, you may feel you are still drowning in a sea of pain from the past. That's how I see the Samaritan woman at the well—until Jesus stepped into her life.

Though I was never a lifeguard, I do have to admit I watched plenty of *Bay Watch* episodes on TV during my teen years. The little that I did learn from that experience is that a drowning person is a dangerous person because their desperate flailing and desire to grab hold of something can also drag down their rescuer. That's why lifeguards are trained to approach victims safely and take control of the situation.

Jesus initially approached the woman with caution, and then quickly took control of the "rescue." He was well aware of her marital history, her pain from the past and the wounds she'd suffered. When He asked her to go get her husband and return, He was bringing these issues to light for the purpose of healing.

Let's take a look at the two most obvious wounds in this woman's life: first, the wound of *racism* and, second, the wound of *relational damage.*

The wound of racism was identified in her statement, *"... How is it that You, being a Jew, ask a drink from me, a Samaritan woman?"* (John 4:9). Clearly, racism has been around for a very long time. It is a tool the enemy uses to inflict degradation and cause separation. But notice that Jesus neither discussed their differences nor got into a racial debate. Instead, He spoke the truth about the essence of who *He* is—the living water.

It is only through Jesus that we find real peace and the answer for all the hatred we see in the world. Jesus is the Prince of Peace, who said, *"Peace I leave with you, My peace I give to you; not as the world gives do I give to you. Let not your heart be troubled, neither let it be afraid"* (John 14:27). We need to draw the peace of God from the One who owns the peace, and then we can share it with the world. Because you can't give what you don't have.

In Paul's letter to the Ephesians, he said, *"Stand therefore, having girded your waist with truth ... and having shod your feet with the preparation of the gospel of peace"* (Ephesians 6:14–15). This word isn't for only a select group of people; it is for *all* believers, *all* races, *all* nationalities. Remember the verse we read earlier: *There is neither Jew nor Greek, there is neither slave nor free, there is neither male nor female; for you are all one in Christ Jesus* (Galatians 3:28).

When the prophet Jeremiah questioned the Lord about the wickedness in the land, the Lord answered him. One line in particular stands out to me: *"Mine heritage is unto me as a speckled bird, the birds round about are against her ..."* (Jeremiah 12:9, KJV). I see that speckled bird as representing the diversity of humanity, made in the image and likeness of God. While racism is a divisive tool of the enemy, diversity is a God-given gift. The Bible says, *Every good and perfect gift is from above, and comes down from the Father of lights, with whom there is no variation or shadow of turning* (James 1:17). We ought to appreciate gifts.

The book of Revelation speaks of people out of every tribe, tongue and nation singing a new song (see Revelation 5:9). How terrible would it be if the only time we sing praises to God with those who are different from us is when we get to heaven? There are no all-white, all-black, all-Hispanic, or all-rich churches in heaven. The authentic Church—the body of Christ—is as diverse and unique as each individual snowflake in a Colorado snowfall.

We are not going to break down the walls of racism by fighting fire with fire; rather, we will bring down those walls by the love and peace that comes through Jesus Christ. Paul described our spiritual war in his letter to the church in Corinth:

> *For though we walk in the flesh, we do not war according to the flesh. For the weapons of our warfare are not carnal but mighty in God for pulling down*

*strongholds, casting down arguments and every high thing that exalts itself against the knowledge of God, bringing every thought into captivity to the obedience of Christ, and being ready to punish all disobedience when your obedience is fulfilled.* (2 CORINTHIANS 10:3-6)

There's no question about it that what our nation and world have gone through lately, and what we are stilling battling, is the same battle Jesus was addressing—the one Paul wrote about, the one Dr. Martin Luther King, Jr. spoke about, and the one many continue to stand up about and declare God's truth over. Racism—an absolute anti-Christ spirit—is another tool of the enemy to separate and divide us, especially since the desire of God is that we love each other as we love ourselves to dwell in unity, be in harmony, working together.

I love to be counted among other great men and women of God who stand against division and speak up for diversity! One of our core values and key pieces of our church is, "appreciate diversity." Because there are lots of people who would say they are not racist, but "you will never see what you fail to teach." And "you will never accomplish what you fail to define!" So don't just have good intentions or short one-time mentions. Teach, preach and define exactly what you believe and know to be true! For we are ALL called to walk in the ministry of reconciliation!

The words Jesus spoke to the Samaritan woman at the well definitely "cast down" arguments, religious tradition, and the wall of pain that had held her captive for years. Her very thoughts were being taken captive to the obedience of

Christ, thus beginning her transition toward her God-given assignment.

The second issue Jesus dealt with was her wound of relational damage. When He asked her to go get her husband, she said she didn't have one. And then even though He seemed to respond with correction, He merely stated the facts (see John 4:17–18). He didn't criticize her or pass judgment on her past; and she confirmed by calling Him a prophet (v. 19).

The Bible says nothing about *why* this woman had had five husbands. Perhaps she was widowed, divorced or a combination of both. Remember, the culture of that day was different from today. For instance, if a Jewish woman's husband died and they had no children, she would marry her husband's brother. Jesus didn't delve into the effects that having five husbands may have had on this woman. She may have suffered great grief. Perhaps she was lied to, cheated on or abandoned. Maybe she was childless, feared yet more loss in her life, and worried how she would be cared for in her latter years. Little did she know that, despite the wounds in her heart, she was about to step into her God-given assignment:

> *... I know that Messiah is coming (who is called Christ). When He comes, He will tell us all things. Jesus said to her, "I who speak to you am He." ... The woman then left her waterpot, went her way into the city, and said to the men, "Come, see a Man who told me all things that I ever did. Could this be the Christ?" Then they went out of the city and came to Him.*

*And many of the Samaritans of that city believed in Him because of the word of the woman who testified, "He told me all that I ever did." So when the Samaritans had come to Him, they urged Him to stay with them; and He stayed there two days. And many more believed because of His own word.* (JOHN 4:25-30, 39-41)

When the Samaritan woman left her waterpot at the well and returned to the city to tell others about Jesus, she literally stepped into her God-given assignment—as an evangelist to take territory! Because of her word, many came to believe Jesus was the Christ—the promised Messiah. In a single day, she went from being a woman who struggled with her past to playing a significant role in her city, forever memorialized in the Scripture. Her test became her testimony.

## FROM THE BUCKET TO THE WELL

I love the symbolism woven throughout the Bible and the metaphorical messages within the stories, placed there for us to discover. In the story of Jesus and the Samaritan woman, let's look at the water bucket she carried and the well of living water—Jesus.

Day after day, the woman went to a well to draw a bucket of literal water to meet her daily needs. Jesus pointed out the obvious, saying, *"Whoever drinks of this water will thirst again"* (John 4:13). And then He identified Himself as a well of living water, which would spring up into everlasting life. In essence, Jesus offered her the opportunity to turn from the bucket to the well as her source of life, health, peace and blessing. Jesus offers us the same opportunity.

Every one of us has a metaphorical bucket that we use to pacify or meet the needs in our lives—the need for healing of the wounds inflicted on us by our experiences. A lot of us even go to church with a "bucket," looking for a smile and quick fill-up—just something that will get us through the day or week.

A bucket mentality and attitude says, "This is what I have to make my life work, and this is just what it will always be like. I'll always be in dysfunctional relationships; I'll always have this obstacle in my path; I'll always have this regret, hurt and pain. I'm not looking for you to change anything, I've got a routine and a rhythm for my rejection, I've got a system in place. I don't need anyone's help!" And the list goes on ...

There was once this rough and gruff man who attended our church; he was always bitter, rude and difficult. And he actually wanted to be a greeter! I told him that I didn't think he could unless he changed the way he talked to people. We had someone new come up to him and ask, "How are you today?" To which he replied, "How does it look—can't you tell?!" Unfortunately, it was that kind of talk and more. Needless to say, he didn't like it when I said he needed to change the way he talked. He wanted to continue to live and talk the way he did because he didn't want to let go of the way he had always been.

People will not only live their literal "bucket life," but they will guard it, protect it, make it look nice and are at times proud of it! I've heard people say things like, "I've been like this as long as I can remember, and I'm still here and doing pretty good." Well, just because that's how you've been, that's how life has been, or that it's just been your reality doesn't mean it needs to stay that way, especially when it comes to your walk with God!

This bucket life, mentality and attitude only pacifies and leaves you wanting and lacking, feeling like you'll always run dry and never stay filled! It's a draining and difficult life, and it makes walking in your significance impossible! People who want to be pacified just want leaders, preachers and teachers to tell them what they want rather than what they actually need! Pacified people stay stuck in their dysfunction rather than break free into their destiny!!

Real satisfaction comes only through Jesus and a close personal relationship with Him. He said, "... *whoever drinks of the water that I shall give him will never thirst. But the water that I shall give him will become in him a fountain of water springing up into everlasting life*" (John 4:14). This means that anytime we need something in our lives—healing, peace, blessing, favor, provision—we can draw from the living water that is Jesus. And this water is available 24/7 because it springs up within us.

Perhaps you realize that you have been masking and pacifying the pain you carry from past wounds. If so, it's time to stop medicating that pain and instead turn and face it. As an act of faith, choose to forgive the one who caused your pain, and then follow Jesus out of that pain. Allow Him to be your well of living water that fully and completely satisfies your every need. When you do, you will then become a well of life for others. That's what happened to the Samaritan woman in our story.

She *left her bucket* and went into the city, where her pain became part of her promise. God turned her situation for her good, and the result of her stepping into her God-given assignment was a revival in her city. You too can experience revival breaking out around you when you get a revelation of just how valuable you are to God and how significant your life is.

Just as I briefly mentioned early on in this chapter about familiar spirits and a strategic attack over your life, the enemy has had an assignment over many people for generations.

I've had some say to me things such as, "Pastor Landon, I struggle with poverty just like my parents did, and my grandparents too." "Pastor, addiction runs in my family." "Well, my grandmother died when she was age 47 and so did my mother. I guess I'll die at that age too." God says, "It's time to be done with the bucket life—come drink from the well of living water."

It's time to be free! It's time to walk into your destiny!

Make the decision to leave the bucket life behind and receive all the healing, peace and provision only Jesus can give. Don't settle for temporary pacification when there's an eternal satisfaction available. Time to drop the bucket! Time to let go and let God bring living water to your life!

Before you read on, take a few moments to pray this prayer:

*Heavenly Father, thank You for Your Word, which is Truth. As we relinquish control of our buckets, which can only pacify, and receive instead the well of living water that is Jesus Christ, I thank You for the healing You now bring.*

*I pray for healing of racial wounds, and the pulling down of the walls that divide us. Forgive us of any wounds we have inflicted on others, as we forgive those who have wounded us. Heal our hearts and heal our nation. Birth within us a ministry of reconciliation through Your gospel of peace.*

*I pray for the healing of relational damage. Holy Spirit, help us to forgive those who have wounded us that we my fully receive the freedom Jesus Christ has obtained for us through His redemptive work on the cross.*

*I pray for a revival of worshippers who will worship You in spirit and truth. And as we receive the revelation of our personal significance, I pray for significant success in our lives as we fulfill our God-given assignments. For Your faithfulness to us and to Your Word, we give you thanks as we pray in Jesus' name. Amen.*

## SIGNIFICANT APPLICATION

||||||||||||||||||||||||||||||||||||||||||||||||||||||||||||||||||||||||||||||||||||||||||||||||||||||||||||||||||||||||||||||||||||

1. Set one alarm a day for each of the magnificent 7 [see page 63] as a reminder to implement each one into your daily and weekly schedule.

_____

_____

_____

_____

2. Discouragement, distraction or making a deal? Which of these three tools have you felt the enemy trying to work in your life the most?

_____

_____

_____

_____

3. What's one thing you can do to combat that tool of the enemy?

_____

_____

_____

_____

**4.** *In what ways have you settled for being pacified instead of satisfied?*

_____

_____

_____

_____

**5.** *Is there a "bucket" in your life that you've been carrying, and what areas of your life has it impacted?*

_____

_____

_____

_____

**6.** *What's a new way you can step out in worship?*

_____

_____

_____

_____

**7.** *Like the woman at the well, how can you help influence others' lives in your community?*

_____

_____

_____

_____

## CHAPTER SIX

# *GOD HAS MORE FOR YOU*

**||**

I always look forward to visiting Capernaum when I'm in Israel. Located in the Galilee of northern Israel, Capernaum was one of the main trading villages in biblical times, as well as a place where Jesus performed some of His recorded miracles, including raising the daughter of Jairus from the dead, casting out a demon from a man, and healing the Roman centurion's servant. Not only was Capernaum Jesus' home base for more than three years, but throughout His ministry He often stayed there, usually with Peter.

Peter's house was located across the street from the synagogue where Jesus taught on a regular basis. In 350 A.D., a Christian church was built on top of Peter's house, and in about 410 A.D., another church was built on top of the first one. Then, in 1990, a beautiful, boat-shaped church with eight pillars was built there—its "hull" situated right over the church built in the 400s. This boat-shaped church symbolizes the many local churches throughout the world where Jesus is actively building the body of Christ, one person at a time.

And when I look at the current church, I remember this exchange between Jesus and His disciples:

> *He said to them, "But who do you say that I am?"*
> *Simon Peter answered and said, "You are the Christ, the son of the living God."*
> *Jesus answered and said to him, "Blessed are you, Simon Bar-Jonah, for flesh and blood has not revealed this to you but My Father who is in heaven. And I also say to you that you are Peter, and on this rock I will build My church, and the gates of Hades shall not prevail against it."* (MATTHEW 16:15-18)

Now as we continue to discover, define and direct our significance, it is vital that we point out this amazing piece of Scripture where Jesus asks his disciples "Who am I?" While we are all trying to define our value, we need to know that Christ was helping the disciples shape who they were by helping them see who He was. Now we all know that the Word was made flesh (see John 1:14) and that God's Word and how we see Jesus shape our lives.

I like to say it like this: When the Word becomes infallible to you, your foundation becomes immovable for you! Because the Word is our foundation, it is our rock upon which we should build our lives! That is why Jesus told Peter "upon that foundation"—that revelation ... that Rock ... I will build my Church; and the gates of hell cannot stand against it (see Matthew 16:18). When you catch the revelation Peter caught, you'll build on the same foundation Peter stood on when he boldly preached the Gospel of Jesus Christ on the Day of Pentecost! Peter's value and significance were established and solidified when He declared the value and significance of Jesus on the earth!

When you go from just knowing Christ to valuing everything about who Jesus is, what He did and what He will do, then shaping your value and what you will do will be much easier! Now that doesn't mean Peter got it all right or did it all perfectly; but it does mean that he was able to be stand in a greater place of significance, value and purpose from that day on. His life still speaks to us all and countless others because he began to define where his significance came from! Ask yourself: Who is Jesus to you—not just who others say He is—but who do *you* say He is? What I'm talking about is a first-hand revelation that is life changing. Second-hand information/revelation is only good not great. It can be helpful, encouraging and even inspiring, but rarely does it last.

The revelation you need to know, declare and walk in is a first-hand revelation of who He is in your life! This may seem intimidating, and I know that because when Jesus asked the disciples that question, they all got quiet except for Peter. I don't know if I'm more impressed by Peter or concerned about the silence of the eleven because that means that only one out of eleven felt confident enough to speak up about who Jesus was to them. Maybe you are afraid of speaking up because you feel like you will get it wrong, or you are intimidated by the question and feel inadequate to answer; or possibly you just simply haven't spent time with Jesus to tell who He is to you.

I want to help speak into your mind and heart because this is a very important piece of your life that needs to be defined and spoken about. If you remain silent on this, it will usually lead to a life of questions and no answers, frustration and no peace, wandering and no direction, and lifelessness and no hope. You must speak up and be bold because a quiet believer is a dying believer. God isn't listening to see if you say it just right, or know enough to declare it, or good enough to back it. No, God looks at your heart (see 1 Samuel 16:7).

You'll learn along the way just like Peter did—who sometimes spoke before he knew and leaped before he looked; but I bet Jesus loved that about Peter because it's easy to coach effort. It's impossible to coach someone who's effortless, motionless and silent—people who want change but won't make changes or people who want help but won't help themselves. It's time to step out in faith like Peter did on multiple occasions, and trust that the Holy Spirit will lead you.

So, what do you know about Jesus? My goal by asking this question is not to draw attention to what you don't know or what you are unclear on, but what you are certain about. What do you know about Jesus to be true and evident in your life? Because when any relationship gets tested, challenged or questioned, you need to go back to what you know: the truth about that person or in this case, Jesus.

The world, the enemy and even you will try to get you to focus on the lies, opinions, negativity, problems and issues; but that's when you need to redirect your mind and heart back to the truth of what you know. Living by this principle helps prevent us from destroying relationships and damaging our own lives. It causes us to go back to a place of truth and trust in key moments just like Peter did. This place of truth and trust is a bold move that will take both courage and humility. As you do take this step, you will begin to define tremendous value in Christ that will also help shape your significance!

The individual building process doesn't stop the moment we make Jesus our Savior and Lord and are added to the body of Christ; rather, God continues to work in each of us to conform us to the very image of Jesus (see Romans 8:29).

It is God's desire that every person who comes to Jesus would experience the victorious life made available for us by His death on the cross. Sometimes this requires us to break through both real and imagined barriers in our lives, which is just what happened in this familiar Bible story that took place in Capernaum.

> *And again he entered Capernaum after some days, and it was heard that He was in the house. Immediately many gathered together, so that there was no longer room to receive them, not even near the door. And He preached the word to them. Then they came to Him, bringing a paralytic who was carried by four men. And when they could not come near Him because of the crowd, they uncovered the roof where He was. So when they had broken through, they let down the bed on which the paralytic man was lying.*
>
> *When Jesus saw their faith, He said to the paralytic, "Son, your sins are forgiven you."*

*And some of the scribes were sitting there and reasoning in their hearts, "Why does this Man speak blasphemies like this? Who can forgive sins but God alone?" But immediately, when Jesus perceived in His spirit that they reasoned thus within themselves, He said to them, "Why do you reason about these things in your hearts? Which is easier, to say to the paralytic, "Your sins are forgiven you," or to say, "Arise, take up your bed and walk"? But that you may know that the Son of Man has power on earth to forgive sins"—He said to the paralytic, "I say to you, arise, take up your bed, and go to your house." Immediately he arose, took up the bed, and went out in the presence of them all, so that all were amazed and glorified God, saying, "We never saw anything like this!"* (MARK 2:1-12)

This story is rich with wisdom and significant truths for us today. I find it again particularly interesting like stories mentioned in previous chapters that the characters are not named in this story either. The paralyzed man was not named, nor were his four friends. A group of scribes (experts on Jewish life and law) were present, but they too went unnamed. Jesus is the only person mentioned by name.

These facts presented in each Bible story are never there by chance. It was not by chance that the man in this story was paralyzed. He could have suffered with a sickness or been bed-ridden with disease, but he was paralyzed. Paralytic people obviously don't have much feeling (in their bodies), which of course is something to take note of because each point has a purpose to reveal more significance to us.

I've known many believers who've admitted that they haven't *felt* God in such a long time that they're not even sure He's real. They don't realize that their words of doubt open a door for the enemy to creep in, saying, "Is God real?" "Is the Bible accurate?" Satan desperately wants to shape people's perspective of God Himself—plus their own value and purpose—because their perspective will shape their world. When I've asked these people how much time they spend with God daily and how often they attend church, many of them say, "Well, my life is really busy with kids, work and taking care of an active household. Sometimes our family just needs to chill on Sunday and watch movies together."

When we allow our perspective to be dictated by movies, the news or social media instead of by prayer and being in His Word, we are going to feel disconnected from God. The Bible says, "*Draw near to God and He will draw near to you ...*" (James 4:8), and *I will set no base or wicked thing before my eyes. I hate the work of them who turn aside [from the right path]; it shall not grasp hold of me* (Psalms 101:3, AMPC). If we want to experience God's presence on a continual basis, then we must stay connected to Him. We must keep our eyes fixed on His Word rather than a screen. For this reason, I took a recent fast from social media.

I did this because I refuse to allow my perspective to be shaped by others—good, bad or indifferent. If I were to allow my perspective to be shaped by others, then they would "own" my perspective. If my perspective is owned by others, then my world is also owned by others! No wonder a lot of us feel like things are out of control—only seeing how all the wrong things are happening or how all the wrong people have power.

When we feel out of control, we fear; and when we fear, we try to control. And when we try to control things, we realize we have no real control, which leads to more fear! Do you see the cycle? Don't let anyone OWN your world, control your perspective or direct your life other than Jesus Christ! For the earth is His footstool; all of it belongs to Him and the fullness thereof! (See Isaiah 66:1, Acts 7:49, Psalms 24:1.) It's no wonder why most Christians are panicking and freaking out; it's because someone other than God is in control.

I can't afford anybody shaping my perspective, funneling into me ideas about what I should preach from the Word of God. I need to hear from Jesus. I need to see what He sees and speak what He speaks rather than parroting what somebody else says. I'm not a puppet, and neither are you! I *chose* to take a break from social media so that I could be healthy in both my mind and heart, and I highly recommend all believers to do the same. It doesn't have to be for 30 days; it could be for one day or perhaps during certain time periods throughout the week.

We've all heard the popular phrase, "We are in this world, but not of it," based on Jesus' prayer for His disciples in which He said, *"They are not of the world, just as I am not of the world"* (John 17:16). As God's people—each one of us significant and valued—we are in the world to carry out our significant assignments from God. But oftentimes, we become so entrenched in the world that we don't know how to get outside of what the world wants us to do. Though we are in the world, we're not to take part in the ways of the world. Instead, we are to change the world.

When I say we are to change the world, I do not mean we are to simply "fix" the world and its many problems. Fixing problems is God's job; our job is to be salt and light wherever we are sent, for Jesus said, *"You are the salt of the earth; but if the salt loses its flavor, how shall it be seasoned? ... You are the light of the world. A city that is set on a hill cannot be hidden"* (Matthew 5:13–14). Salt can only preserve something that exists; therefore, we are here to salt what God has established.

We are also here to shine upon and give light to the things God has done. Though our individual assignments are unique and many, within those assignments we are to be salt and light in this world. This is the reason we must be careful in what we allow to shape our individual worlds. If I let others shape my world, they will also shape my words; and that's how our conversations usually lead to something negative, dark and full of doubt. But if I am letting God and His Word shape my perspective, then I see that He holds the world and He directs my words!

I was recently talking to a friend who only seemed to want to see and feel the negative, fearful and doubtful. The hard part was that I could totally understand where he was coming from and could have easily just sympathized and agreed with him. But since I'd been fasting media and meditating on God's words and promises, I kept redirecting the conversation back to the hopeful! He brought up something about China and then Russia, and I said, "Well, thank God we don't belong to the kingdoms of this world but to an eternal kingdom that will rule and reign forever!" And he would begin to change just a little and say something like "Yeah, I guess."

Then the conversation turned to vaccines, COVID-19, masks, and I said, "Well, thank You Jesus that He is our protector, healer and physician!" And he replied, "Yeah, you're right." By the end of the conversation, he told me how encouraging it was to be around someone of hope and faith! Now, this man has been living for Jesus for a long time! So it wasn't like he didn't know the truth, or had never heard what I've said before. It was simply that he had placed himself in a position where he hadn't heard or felt God. He had surrounded and filled himself with a wrong perspective, and it had literally shaped his world. He was distant, disconnected and paralyzed—unable to see clearly, or feel or hear God; this man was frozen in fear with no hope or faith, wondering if things would ever get better.

Have you ever felt like that and in need of someone speaking into your heart from a godly perspective? Or maybe you know a friend or family member who's like my friend, and you now need to be the messenger of good news. Whichever side you are on, you know what to do. Go get around that person you've been avoiding because you know they will tell you what you need rather than what you want. If you are supposed to be the messenger, then go speak over that friend and family member with hope, faith, love, peace and grace. Get a new word; get a new world!

## JESUS IN THE HOUSE

I can imagine the nameless paralyzed man in Mark 2, who had little or no feeling in his body, wondering if his life mattered, if God even heard him. Perhaps when some, who had gathered outside the house to hear Jesus, saw this paralyzed man being carried by four of his friends, they may have thought they weren't as significant either, thinking, *His issue is much bigger than mine, so I'll just shrink back.* This happens so much in church. People see others and think others deserve more, need more, or that they are more important, valuable or significant. They begin to see and believe that God wants to help, heal and bless everyone else but them. They watch everyone get their miracle and are left with a hope unmet.

From God's perspective, neither the paralyzed man nor those who may have shrunk back were any more or less significant than anyone else in attendance that day. Jesus was in the house; He was there for anyone and everyone who needed His touch.

Jesus is no longer subject to the constraints of time and space of this life. For those of us who have made Him Savior and Lord, Jesus is always in the house because He now lives *in* us. He is present for each of us at church, at home, on a morning jog or at work. He is here with me, and He is here with you. He will never leave you, and He will never forsake you (see Hebrews 13:5).

This would be a great time to take a praise break or shout "Amen!" Because this should get anyone fired up! This right here is a preacher's bread and butter—to simply declare that "He is in the house!" When worry creeps in, He is in the house with you! When you're driving and fear tries to grip you, "He is in the car!" When you are at the office, fighting off insecurity, "He is in your office!" No matter what you are facing or what the odds look like, no matter where you are seated—whether in the cheap seats or in the front row—God is in the house! And if He is in the house, then your miracle is in the house!

## CARRY OR CURB

Even though we find ourselves at times living in a state of separation from God, there are people around us who can see our value, who know God has more for us, and are willing to carry us when we are in a seemingly impossible situation. The hard part is, sometimes we just need to admit that we need to be carried.

If the paralyzed man could have had his way, he may well have gone back to the place where his bed mat was usually placed so that he could beg. Lying on his mat and begging by the curb was what he was accustomed to. Begging was what he knew—a comfortable and familiar situation that enabled him to "get by." But God had something more for him, and his friends knew that "something more" could come only from Jesus. His four friends may have well said, "Although he is paralyzed, we know his potential; and we know God has more for him. We are going to carry him to Jesus."

We all have times when we need to be carried by other believers who are willing to stand in the gap for us in prayer, speak God's truth to us when we need to hear it, and boldly carry us from our curb to Jesus so that we can take up our beds and walk on our own. But to receive all God has for us, we must be willing to let go of the worldly mindsets and perceptions we've allowed to affect us in a negative manner and instead be willing to be carried from our point of pain to our place of change!

In other words, we need to sit at the feet of Jesus and listen for His voice through His Word. What is comfortable and familiar to you—the curb that says you will never leave this place, and life can never be better? Maybe it's an old job, city or environment. Maybe you've been limited by who you think you are vs. who He created you to be. Maybe that old comfortable mat is the old talents, abilities and skills you've always leaned on, and God is about to call you into a greater dimension to see that you have more than you thought. If it is indeed true that our perspective shapes our world, then it is also true that the familiar can shape our future.

Now if the familiar is anything less than God's best, then your future will always fall short of your hopes and expectations. BUT, if you can create a new familiar—a healthy, strong and bright familiar, then you can shape a bright and beautiful future! You just have to allow yourself to be carried sometimes when you can't carry yourself. When you allow the right people in your life to sometimes take charge and say, "We are going to carry you through this," then you end up being taken to your place of transformation.

Let me put it like this: When your kids don't "feel like" going to church, it's time to carry them. When your friend, who's battling depression, doesn't want to go to prayer ministry, carry them. When you are stuck in a rut, it's time to let some friends pick you up off your old curb and carry you! No vote required, no debate over it—just pick you up and take you to Jesus! I pray you have that kind of people around you as well as become that kind of person for someone else and carries you when you need it!

The book of Proverbs says that this kind of person is not just there for good times but for times of adversity (see Proverbs 17:17). I thank God for friends who carried me when I needed it. I praise Jesus for parents who made me go to church when I didn't want to. I have the testimony I have because someone carried me! Don't ever be too proud for someone to carry you, and don't ever be afraid to carry someone even when they don't like it. I am more concerned about those who didn't have a friend to carry them or refused because of their pride to let someone carry them. I wonder how many paralyzed people are sitting by the curb of life just watching it all pass by because they wouldn't let someone carry them. You, your family and your friends are too significant to God and His purpose for you in this world to be left on the curb and not be carried!

## *AS ONE*

Now carrying is one thing; carrying in the right direction is another. Let's consider the four men in our Bible story who carried their paralyzed friend. Remember, it is the handful of people closest to us who will determine our destinies—good or bad. Their words and actions will either create a ceiling of doubt above us or they will raise our faith. What if each of those men (reasonably assuming they were the paralytic's closest friends) had grabbed a corner of the bed mat and decided to go his own direction? How fast would that mat have dropped? Real fast! We may laugh at the idea, but when it comes to trusting our friends to carry us, things like this happen all the time. If we've not been deliberate in choosing who we allow to get close to us, the people we depend on the most will oftentimes try to drag us in different directions. They will either direct us to Jesus or drag us away from Him.

I've also seen this happen many times: Believers who are not careful about who they spend time with or who they listen to can allow themselves to be pulled in different directions. Then they become frustrated with the people around them. They wonder why they feel confused, misdirected and tugged back and forth. What they need is the right friends who will stand in faith with them and take them in the right direction— to Jesus! That's just what the paralyzed man's four friends did. Maybe you have friends pulling you toward another vacation, to spend more time at the gym or to go to parties all the time. But then maybe you have one friend actually pulling you to Jesus. Which friend will succeed? The painful part is that I usually see people cut out the last friend first. When people feel busy, church is the first thing to go.

When people feel pulled in multiple directions, the godly influence is dismissed first. The truth behind this is that we tend to be harsher with the people who we know will forgive and love us the most. How much better would life be if we just had the right people pulling us into the right direction in the same way? Don't cut out the one person who's trying to pull you the right way. And if you can get them all going the same way, great! If not, recruit three new friends.

One of my favorite movies is *Gladiator*, and one of the best scenes in the movie is when they are fighting in The Colosseum and Maximus starts commanding all of the gladiators to move "as one." But these guys are not all on the same team; in fact, they fight only for themselves. Some of them had fought with Maximus when he was the commander of the armies of the north, and some even had begun to be loyal to Maximus since his captivity. But they were all used to fighting separately and in their own way.

Now in this specific fight, all of these gladiators were going up against a whole different group. Maximus knew the only way to win—and more importantly stay alive—was to fight together. So he directed his team with one commanding phrase: "As one!" At first, one of the gladiators wasn't listening but doing his own thing. Consequently, he lost his life, but the rest gathered together in the center of the arena and began to fight "as one." The more they worked together in the same direction with the same goal, the more they won. Eventually, they won the battle, and overcame all odds because everyone worked "as one."

You need everyone who has a hand in your life, to work "as one." You need everyone who you are doing life with to fight "as one." There's no time to risk "getting dropped" for going in multiple directions with different visions, plans, goals and leadership. It's time for one direction and one vision.

## *BREAKTHROUGH*

The paralytic's friends knew just where he needed to go, and so they carried him directly to the house where Jesus was teaching that day. Imagine their surprise when they encountered so great a crowd that they couldn't even get near the entry door. But they didn't allow the circumstances to prevent them from getting to Jesus. They simply climbed up to the top of the house and broke through the roof.

I can imagine what those four friends might have thought when they arrived and couldn't get to the entry door: "We've just carried this man for six miles under the blazing sun, and we're not going back until we get him to Jesus!" And then I wonder how many others may have simply given up, saying, "Well, I guess getting him to Jesus today just wasn't meant to be."

While walking in God's purpose for my life, I've learned not to give up just because I encounter a closed door; instead, I start looking for the next door. I simply say, "God, this closed door doesn't mean that I don't have a purpose; it means I need to find another way." We need to be willing to fight for our purpose.

The paralytic's friends were willing to fight for their friend's purpose. Perhaps their conversation went something like this: "Hey, if we can't get him in the door, maybe we can lower him through the roof. But let's not tell him what we're planning just yet." I envision them leaving their friend lying on his mat while they climbed up to the roof and broke through the branches and mud plaster—the standard materials used in that day. Once they'd broken through, they had to secure ropes so that they could lower their friend. They were willing not only to carry him, but also to fight for him so that he could get his breakthrough.

Perhaps you need a breakthrough in a particular area of your life right now. Maybe your friends are standing with you, pointing you to Jesus. Or maybe you are on your own in your faith walk and are discouraged because a door you expected to open slammed shut. Don't accept the old religious attitude that says, "Oh, well, it must not have been God's will." No! That closed door can either defeat you or it can strengthen your resolve to push forward and fight for your breakthrough. But, are you willing to climb higher and get your hands dirty?

God is saying, "When you find the front door is closed, then know I have a higher way for you. You'll find that way right before you if only you're willing to go the route that nobody else has gone. When you do, you'll go higher than others have gone and seen things no one else has seen."

Sadly, not everyone who loves Jesus is willing to make the faith climb to get to their breakthrough. They're not willing to take the time required to pray, to go the extra mile, or to get their hands dirty working for their breakthrough. Some may say, "Well, the Bible says the just live by faith, and so I'm just believing God to answer my prayer." Of course we are to live by faith, but the Bible also says, *"Thus also faith by itself, if it does not have works, is dead"* (James 2:17).

In Paul's letter to Timothy, whom he considered his son in the faith, said, *"Fight the good fight of faith ..."* (1 Timothy 6:12). Faith is a fight, and we need to fight for our breakthroughs. We need to surround ourselves with others who will fight for us.

You may say, "But, I don't have the kind of friends who will fight for me, who will carry me to Jesus." Then be to someone else what you want others to be to you. Be the one to fight for someone else, to carry them to Jesus. You'll never build an army if you wait for others to come sign up to fight with you. You build an army of people by first going to fight for them.

It's easy to give up when fighting isn't convenient and when doors slam shut. It's even easier to chalk up a disappointment to closed doors being God's will. Sometimes we just need to make a door to our breakthrough. We need to declare in faith, "I'm going to find a way to Jesus." "I'm going to find a way for my marriage." "I'm going to see a change in my finances." Our attitude should be, "Although it's been a long time since I've felt the touch of God in my life, I won't stop here. I'm going to fight for my breakthrough because I'm significant, and God's assignment on my life is significant."

When I was nine years old and the doctors told my parents that I may never speak again following the accident that knocked out part of my trachea, my dad prayed all night. "God, You can heal my son, and I'm not leaving here until You do." Because my dad was willing to fight for my breakthrough, when I woke up the very next morning, I'd been miraculously healed. Although I was unable to speak, my dad and the other men from our church carried me to the feet of Jesus, just as the paralytic's friends in Mark 2 carried him. Since then, I've had to fight for my ministry, fight for my marriage, fight for the ability to have children, fight for my friends and family. I've also had people continue to fight for me, for Emily, and for Adelé! Whether it's climbing higher, getting your hands dirty and digging out a new way, or pulling down strongholds to see a breakthrough, this life is not going to just happen the way you think it will.

The paralytic man's story contains three doors: the one that was blocked, the one the friends made through the roof, and the One sitting in the house named Jesus. That means that one of the three doors in your life will be blocked and unable to open; another door will need to be made by you; and the other door will always open for you. So, when you see a door in your life, you just need to assess what kind of door it is. Because we know what Scripture says about doors: Knock, and it will be opened to you (see Matthew 7:7). Don't be discouraged by closed doors; there's a better door. Don't be afraid to make an open door—you might just see a breakthrough. Then be ready to receive all that God has for you with the open door in front of you.

## INTERNAL AND EXTERNAL

The Bible says, *When Jesus saw their faith, He said to the paralytic, "Son, your sins are forgiven you"* (Mark 2:5). We don't know the man's name, but Jesus certainly did. Yet He called the man His own son. Jesus forgave the internal to change the external. An external healing will never heal the internal; however, an internal transformation will bring about an external change in a person's life. We oftentimes pray, asking God to help us with external matters when we should instead ask Him to first heal what's on the inside, in our hearts.

The heart of mankind has always been important to God. For instance, when He instructed the prophet Samuel to anoint the young David as king, He said, "... *For the* LORD *does not see as man sees; for man looks at the outward appearance, but the* LORD *looks at the heart*" (1 Samuel 16:7). Likewise, Jesus first looked at the heart of the paralytic and declared his sins forgiven before He ever told him to rise and walk. This is the heart of the reason for writing this book, because so many people look for external things to bring significance to their lives. But our significance does not come from the external but internal. External things can produce success at different points and seasons in our lives that are only temporal, but a touch of significance in the deepest part of who we are is eternal.

What if Jesus had commanded him to stand without first having given the paralytic the strength to do so by forgiving his sins? Jesus first had to heal him on the inside. It's what gave him the faith and strength to stand. Imagine being paralyzed and never using those muscles; they would be weak and in atrophy. Even if your legs were able to move again, they wouldn't have the muscle strength and internal power to stand up and walk! Jesus knew He needed to take care of what people can't see so they can be blessed by what they do see. That's how He works in our lives inside first, outside second. I say it like this: Your private wins will determine your public victories.

This is what God did with David the shepherd boy, who became a great warrior and then a great king. When he was in the field, he had to fight a lion and a bear to protect his sheep before he fought Goliath. Even when he showed up to fight Goliath, he told King Saul that he had defeated a lion and a bear. It was after telling him, that he had enough confidence to let him fight Goliath. Now the battle against Goliath was in front of the armies of Israel and the Philistines, but the fight for the sheep against the lion and the bear were private victories.

This means that your private battles need to be fought and won before your public ones can be won. It's the internal before the external—the private before the public, It's the issues of the heart before the miracle in your hand and dealing with the iniquity before healing the infirmity. And it all begins inside with the deepest parts of who you are—that's where your healing begins then your value can transcend. Jesus wants to heal the internal so He can change the external. Will you let Him? No one else but him can see or fix what's on the inside of us. He is our healer and physician, so let Him begin a good work in you and establish healing, strength, power, love and significance because He who began a good work will finish is faithful to finish!

Look at when Jesus saw the faith of the four that He forgave the sin of the one, which is interesting in the light of an Old Testament verse that says, *He will even deliver one who is not innocent; yes, he will be delivered by the purity of your hands* (Job 22:30). We can't read this story about Jesus and the paralytic without seeing how our faith can impact someone else's eternity. We can choose to either devalue and make insignificant the level of faith and influence we have, or we can demonstrate our faith by carrying others to Jesus, showing them who He is. We don't have to fix all the problems in the world; we are called to simply reach the world for Jesus. That's how we will see things change; it's how we make disciples.

The story of Jesus and the paralytic is also told in the Gospels of Matthew and Luke. Luke gives us a little additional information in that he says not only were scribes present that day, but *that there were Pharisees and teachers of the law sitting by, who had come out of every town of Galilee, Judea, and Jerusalem ...* (Luke 5:17). Again, the Pharisees were the religious leaders who believed in, and strictly adhered to, the traditions handed down from their religious predecessors, and they expected the same of everyone else. As always, Jesus confronted their tradition with Truth when He said to the paralytic, "[*Son*], *your sins are forgiven you*" (v. 20).

> *And the scribes and the Pharisees began to reason, saying, "Who is this who speaks blasphemies? Who can forgive sins but God alone?"*
>
> *But when Jesus perceived their thoughts, He answered them and said to them, "Why are you reasoning in your hearts? Which is easier, to say, Your sins are forgiven you, or to say, Rise up and walk? But that you may know the Son of Man has power on earth to forgive sins"—He said to the man who was paralyzed, "I say to you, arise, take up your bed, and go to your house."*
>
> *Immediately he rose up before them, took up what he had been lying on, and departed to his own house, glorifying God. And they were all amazed, and they glorified God and were filled with fear, saying, "We have seen strange things today."* (LUKE 5:21-26)

When Jesus spoke the words, "Your sins are forgiven you," He already knew He was about to win an argument that was never spoken forth. Just as God looks at the heart of man, so

Jesus perceived the hearts of the scribes and Pharisees as they reasoned according to their manmade laws and traditions. He essentially called them out in front of all who were there that day, and then He commanded the paralytic to arise, pick up his bed and go home. The argument was over before it had even begun, and then the celebration began followed right after.

Throughout the Gospels we read about Jesus' encounters with the scribes and Pharisees, in which He called them names such as blind guides, fools, whitewashed tombs, serpents, vipers and hypocrites. I find it interesting in the story of the paralytic that while Jesus called them out and revealed their hearts, He didn't rebuke them as in other instances. Instead, He essentially said, "I want to show you that I have the authority to forgive sins. I'm going to heal this man so that you can see I don't care only for him and his four friends, but I care about the hearts of everyone here today, even those who oppose me. I want to heal the hearts of those who are in confusion, whose minds are being torn and tormented, who suffer under the weight of sin. I am going to show you that I'm here for all of you."

Jesus is here for all of us just as He was for those who had gathered in and around the house in Capernaum that day. He wants to heal our hearts and free us from the confines of the self-made comfort zones that have held us captive— sometimes for years. Sadly, we are reluctant to step out of our comfort zones because they are familiar. We are more comfortable living with the pain and wounds from the past than facing the possibility of experiencing new wounds if we step out and do something we've never done before. We choose the tyranny of the familiar over the promise of freedom.

But the paralytic man made up his mind to turn his back on the familiar and the comfort of his mat that day. Though his friends had carried him to Jesus, he had to use his own faith, in essence saying, "I'm not going to live like this anymore. I refuse to be paralyzed by anger, bitterness, unforgiveness and insecurity." And with that, he stood up.

Not only did Jesus command him to stand, but He also said, "Take up your bed and go to your house." (see v. 24). Why would Jesus tell him to do that? His bed mat was representative of the place known for all his shortcomings, hurts, pains and the pitiful conditions in which he lived. Jesus didn't want him to merely walk away from his past, but to simply leave it behind. He wanted him to use it as his testimony.

I too used to be paralyzed, not physically but emotionally. I was an angry man, a jealous man, sick and lame on the inside. But today I am a free man because of the grace of Jesus Christ. I haven't forgotten my past; rather, I now use it as my testimony. If God can do this for me, He can also do it for you.

In Luke's account of Jesus and the paralytic man, he described the setting, saying, "... *And the power of the Lord was present to heal them*" (Luke 5:17). This fact is important because it indicates that just because the power was present, there was no guarantee that healing was automatic. Those who wanted healing were responsible for their own breakthroughs. Everyone gathered in and around the house that day had *chosen* to fight for their healing—or in the case of the paralytic man, his friends had chosen to fight for him. Though Jesus had the power to heal, He did not force it on anyone.

Jesus said, *"I am with you always, even to the end of the age"* (Matthew 28:20), which means He is present with you right now. Therefore, the power to heal is present to heal you as well. Perhaps you need physical healing, or, like the paralytic man, you need an internal healing of the heart. If you've made Jesus your Lord and Savior, then your sins are forgiven. All you need to do to receive your breakthrough healing is to simply step out in faith. Take a few moments to raise your hands to the Lord and make this declaration:

*I declare in the name of Jesus that the power to heal is present with me at this moment, right now. Where there once was doubt, there is now faith. Where there once was uncertainty, I now have clarity. Where there once was confusion, there is now peace and resolve. I receive my complete and total healing—spirit, soul, and body—and I thank You for it, Lord. I praise You that I am significant in Your eyes, and that You have created and prepared me for the significant assignment that is mine and mine alone.*

*I receive all that You have for me, and I praise You for it in Jesus' name. Amen.*

## SIGNIFICANT APPLICATION

1. *What influences are shaping your world?*

   _____

   _____

   _____

   _____

2. *Who has carried you in your time of need?*

   _____

   _____

   _____

   _____

3. *Who have you carried and why? Are you ready to carry someone else?*

   _____

   _____

   _____

   _____

4. *Thinking of your top (three) friends, which direction are they each pulling you?*

   _____

   _____

   _____

   _____

**5.** *How can you get everyone working as one in your life?*

_____

_____

_____

_____

**6.** *Name three internal battles you need to win.*

_____

_____

_____

_____

**7.** *List one giant in your life that needs to fall and for everyone to see.*

_____

_____

_____

_____

## CHAPTER SEVEN
# *COMMANDING FAITH*

## II

Is there someone you know or look up to that is just "that person" who when they walk into a room, they are now in charge; or when everyone is waiting for a word or answer, they are the one everyone is waiting on? There's something about a commanding presence and posture with some people that is so appealing and intriguing. It's like James Bond walking into a room with one of his famous tuxedos on; it's Wonder Woman marching in with her trademark music. To be able to walk with such a powerful demeanor and posture, to carry yourself in such a way that you can change the atmosphere of a room, office, home, school or situation is a necessary piece for everyone seeking significance.

So it then begs the question, can anyone become "that person" and walk in a commanding place of faith that changes things? Now it's more than words, more than posture or cadence to your stride. It's a depth within a person and a resolve of who they are and what they have to offer.

Have there been any points in your life that you had a commanding presence and power about you? Or is there a time that you wish you had been more in charge and control? Most of the time, it's the latter. For instance, after a difficult confrontation, we usually say, "I should have said ..." or "I wish I would have ..."; or we come up with the perfect line or thing to do after the fact, leaving us wishing we could rewind time or pause time to gather our thoughts and do or say what we only wish we would have in that missed moment. I've had a ton of moments like these, but I don't think Jesus EVER had one because let's face it: He's Jesus! But I know the disciples did and so did others.

But there were times in the Bible that I read the response of how some people interacted and responded that make me think, "Wow, what a great comeback!" Like the time Jesus told the woman who came begging Him to heal and deliver her daughter. He called her a *dog* because she was a Gentile! But she responded perfectly by saying but even the dogs get scraps from the master's table! (see Matthew 15:22–28). Boom! That was an amazing response because she didn't respond with her frustration and offense. She responded powerfully and truthfully in the moment and Jesus was so moved by it He did exactly what she asked Him for! Moments like that blow me away because most people, like me, would be furious and only say things I regretted and leave wishing I would have said something different or done something different. This woman had a commanding faith about her; she was bold and courageous! Maybe it was the desperation talking or the "mother bear" in her coming out; or maybe it was just the power of knowing who she was and being so comfortable in it that she could walk boldly up to the Prince of Peace and speak so truthfully. Either way, it was a commanding moment.

I wasn't always about being so quick in the moment and having a good comeback, and sometimes I'm still not. Now it's not about just being quick and having just anything to say, but in this life as a believer, it's about having something faith filled to say—a significant truth with timing and power.

Jesus made an interesting statement at the conclusion of His parable of the persistent widow. He said, *"Nevertheless, when the Son of Man comes, will He really find faith on the earth?"* (Luke 18:8). The subject of faith was often brought up when Jesus interacted with people. For instance, when His disciples thought they would die at sea during a storm, He said they had "little faith." In another instance he described a man as having "great faith." Clearly, faith was—and is—important to the Lord.

Most of us are familiar with Hebrews 11:1: *Now faith is the substance of things hoped for, the evidence of things not seen.* And in verse 6, we read these words: *"But without faith it is impossible to please Him, for he who comes to God must believe that He is, and that He is a rewarder of those who diligently seek Him."*

Let's take a look at two Bible stories—one from the Old Testament and one from the New Testament—which both illustrate examples of what I refer to as *commanding faith*. In the first story, we find Joshua and all the mighty men of valor about to defend the Israelites from the enemy armies.

*And the LORD said to Joshua, "Do not fear them, for I have delivered them into your hand; not a man of them shall stand before you." Joshua therefore came upon them suddenly, having marched all night from Gilgal. So the LORD routed them before Israel, killed them with a great slaughter at Gibeon, chased them along the road that goes to Beth Horon, and struck them down as far as Azekah and Makkedah. And it happened, as they fled before Israel and were on the descent of Beth Horon, that the LORD cast down large hailstones from heaven on them as far as Azekah, and they died. There were more who died from the hailstones than the children of Israel killed with the sword.*

*Then Joshua spoke to the LORD in the day when the LORD delivered up the Amorites before the children of Israel, and he said in the sight of Israel: "Sun, stand still over Gibeon; and Moon, in the Valley of Aijalon." So the sun stood still, and the moon stopped, till the people had revenge upon their enemies.*

*Is this not written in the Book of Jasher? So the sun stood still in the midst of heaven, and did not hasten to go down for about a whole day. And there has been no day like that, before it or after it, that the LORD heeded the voice of a man; for the LORD fought for Israel.*

(JOSHUA 10:8-14)

Notice the final verse above says the Lord heeded the voice of a man, a human being. It doesn't say He heeded the voice of a great man of God—one much better, stronger, more talented and more anointed than others. Joshua was described only as "a man."

Now let's go to the New Testament and the story of a Roman centurion's encounter with Jesus:

> *Now when [Jesus] concluded all His sayings in the hearing of the people, He entered Capernaum. And a certain centurion"s servant, who was dear to him, was sick and ready to die. So when he heard about Jesus, he sent elders of the Jews to Him, pleading with Him to come and heal his servant. And when they came to Jesus, they begged Him earnestly, saying that the one for whom He should do this was deserving, "for he loves our nation, and has built us a synagogue."*
>
> *Then Jesus went with them. And when He was already not far from the house, the centurion sent friends to Him, saying to Him, "Lord, do not trouble Yourself, for I am not worthy that You should enter under my roof. Therefore I did not even think myself worthy to come to You. But say the word, and my servant will be healed. For I also am a man placed under authority, having soldiers under me. And I say to one, 'Go,' and he goes; and to another 'Come,' and he comes; and to my servant, 'Do this,' and he does it."*
>
> *When Jesus heard these things, He marveled at him, and turned around and said to the crowd that followed Him, "I say to you, I have not found such great faith, not*

*even in Israel!" And those who were sent, returning to the house, found the servant well who had been sick.*
(LUKE 7:1-10)

Joshua and the Roman centurion both walked upon the earth in vastly different time periods, yet they had one thing in common: their *commanding faith.* I want to point out several truths buried within the account of the centurion's encounter with Jesus. First, the Jews who asked Jesus to heal the centurion's servant described him as a generous man, saying he loved the Jews and had built them a synagogue. Generosity will always open doors in our lives, though we may not know which door is going to open. Generosity always begets generosity.

Now I'm no Robert Morris; and I say that because his book *The Blessed Life* is so powerful and filled with stories about how God used him to be generous, and then God in turn was generous towards him in tremendous and wonderful ways. So I'm not trying to compete with that, but I am compelled to share how God has worked in my life in this area. Now as you read about my story and other people's stories of how God worked in us, don't let it be a point of discouragement and say "I've never seen anything like that." Instead, I dare you to look and see how God truly has worked in your life.

When we first started our church in 2018, we didn't have much and could afford less. But we knew we should start a missions department that could send people on trips, send financial support around to areas that the Lord began to show us, and pray for the nations and believe that God would help us reach the lost. Well, our first missions area was just south of the border in Mexico with My360 project, a sustainable missions program built around making shoes for children in third-world countries who didn't have any. The shoe is very cool, like a moccasin, and grows with the child; my friend Darryl Carnley is the founder of My360, and I was excited to partner with him.

We immediately saw that they needed a van for the people who were working and serving at this wonderful mission. So our church decided to sow into the ministry by purchasing a van. It was wonderful—a great van and was used a lot! Now at the same time, our church was growing and needed a church van for ourselves. But after we gave this van away, another church donated a church van to us! (It gets better!) Since we launched our missions program in 2018, God has opened the door for more missions opportunities, and we have been able to plant over 120 churches in three countries, partnering with My360 and The Movement International! Now that's huge—especially for a three-year-old church!

Generosity has been the key to unlocking these opportunities, and it is the same key to unlock new potential in your life, purpose and significance! Give when it hurts, give when it's not easy, give when they least expect it, give generously, give joyfully, give thankfully, give sacrificially, and give in every opportunity because your generosity will open doors in your life! The Kingdom of God moves at the pace of generous believers, so if you want to reach the world, then start giving! If you aren't tithing to your local church yet, then start today. If doors have been closing around you, start giving to people close to you, and watch God open doors and do the unexpected.

A second buried truth from this story is that the centurion did not consider himself worthy for Jesus to come to his house, yet he had absolute faith that if Jesus merely said the word his servant would be healed. Jesus was amazed that this man, a citizen of Rome, showed what Jesus described as "great faith."

Now there are only a couple times in Jesus' ministry when He was amazed by someone, and this was one of them. And if Jesus was amazed, then we ought to pay attention! We are amazed by God's grace, but He can be amazed by our faith—not by our goodness, talents, abilities, intellect or pedigree but by our faith. If that doesn't get you motivated for great faith, then I don't know what will because when I hear that God can be amazed by my decision to exercise faith, I just get fired up and want to step out—no, JUMP out in crazy faith! Just a word of faith can make a huge difference in your life.

When was the last time you can say you stepped out and amazed God by your faith? God has never been pleased by safe living and small thinking because those are the antithesis of great commanding faith. When we are trying to find our significance, we need to understand that it may not take much; it may only take a few words to change everything! Sometimes it's "Be healed!"; "Lazarus, come forth!"; or "This is My Son in whom I am well pleased" that can change the trajectory of your life!

Maybe it's God saying that you are loved, you are His child, son, or daughter, or that He has a plan and hope for you. Maybe you have been looking for an event to help shape your life, value or significance; but sometimes it's just a word from our heavenly Father. It may come through one of His servants like through a parent, pastor, leader, or friend, God can use any of his servants to send His Word. However He chooses to send it, be ready, expecting and waiting because God wants to speak a defining, life-changing, and significant word over your life! We all have had plenty of negative words spoken over us, but what about the powerful life-changing words? (You'll have a chance to reflect and think about this at the end of the chapter.) The enemy would rather us only think about the bad, but consider Paul's words in Philippians 4:8:

> *Finally, brothers and sisters, whatever is true,*
> *whatever is noble, whatever is right, whatever is pure,*
> *whatever is lovely, whatever is admirable—if anything is*
> *excellent or praiseworthy—think about such things.* (NIV)

The third buried truth is that the centurion remains nameless in this story. Jesus was amazed at the man's great faith, yet his name is not remembered. As believers, many of us walk through life wondering if our lives and work are significant, or if we are really making a positive impact on this world and a difference in the lives of others. I'm here to tell you the answer is *yes!* You and I have great significance and great worth. *Unnamed* is what I thought about titling this book, since so many significant stories in the Bible tell of nameless people and it happens all throughout history because it's not just those in the spotlight, on TV, in a book or with a title who make a difference. It's the people who go unnoticed at times, unnamed and unsung.

Those unnamed people had huge significance in the Bible and were significant to Jesus. I don't mind if I go my whole life as unknown to everyone else, as long as I am known by Him! Jesus found the unnamed woman at the well significant, He found the centurion significant, He found the lame man, the blind man, the Shunammite woman and so many more significant. Unnamed heroes make up the majority of history and our world, while a short list sometimes dominates the headlines. Unnamed heroes don't look for the credit, they don't want the attention and aren't self-serving. Our amazing world is made up of billions of amazing people whose names you do not know—or may never know.

Maybe you feel like one of the "unnamed" because your work, job or occupation isn't a "big deal"—that it's unimportant or insignificant. This can cause some major difficulties in people's lives especially when trying to define and direct your significance! No matter what your occupation is, you have significance. Jesus was a carpenter, Matthew a tax collector, Peter a fisherman, Paul a tent maker; others were shepherds, boat makers, politicians, and entrepreneurs, etc. They all worked those jobs and made huge impacts in people's lives. Your occupation is more than just a job; it is a position of influence, and it plays an integral part in God's plan for your life and in His Kingdom! You could be a janitor or a judge, a preacher or a principal, an athlete or an artist, an executive or an elected official.

Don't discredit where you are and what you do. Never say "Well, all I do is ..." or "God can't use me, I'm just a ..." No matter what position it is, where it is or how high or low you may feel on the ladder of success, God can use you and what you are doing to impact the world around you. Sometimes you will see your impact; the rest of the time you won't know who or how, but you are making an impact even if your job doesn't even come in direct contact with other people.

Now if you don't like what you do, then you need to do one of two things: 1) Be faithful and content with what you do, or 2) Change what you do. Take a leap of faith and start a new career, direction or path to pursue what you desire. But whatever you do, do it with all you've got and with a spirit of excellence, because you can find contentment in where you are. First Timothy 6:6 says, *But godliness with contentment is great gain.* Let's face it: If you hate what you do or where you are, it's pretty tough to find value, significance and peace in your life! Otherwise, you will live in a state of constant frustration and disappointment. So, make a decision: Step into the position God has for you, and live out His significant purpose He created you for.

We see a fourth buried truth in the story of the nameless centurion in a demonstration of faith through leadership. As a Roman centurion, this officer was a part of a legion with 6,000 and put in charge of a military unit of 100 legionaries. He was also responsible for issues within in his home, as evidenced by his calling for Jesus to heal his servant. As a pastor, I've learned that any specific issue remains a single problem until the leader refuses to deal with it. If the problem is not dealt with, the leader then becomes the problem.

But this wonderful man in our story made the decision to deal with the issue in his home. He sent elders of the Jews to ask Jesus to heal his servant. I can imagine the man must have been looking through his window and, upon seeing Jesus coming toward his home and feeling unworthy, he sent his friends to Him with a new idea: "Just say the word and my servant will be healed."

As leaders in our own homes, we must take the necessary steps to address issues that arise in our home through faith-filled leadership. We must take ownership and responsibility for the areas of authority that God has given us, not neglecting what is under our care. I see people struggle with this all the time because it's much easier to address other peoples' problems rather than our own because those issues are personal. It's always more comfortable to talk about someone else's problems rather than our own. Anytime I see people trying to fix other people's problems and take control of other situations outside of their own authority, it's usually because they are unable or unwilling to face their own issues, which is within their own responsibility.

Like at church, when a parent tries to control the way the youth group is being run or demand that the children's team operate a certain way—it is usually because they can't control the areas that they should. But the centurion wasn't trying to control things outside of his realm of authority and get mad at Jesus; he was taking ownership of what he could, simply showing healthy faith-filled leadership and believing

Jesus only needed to send His word. If it's under your roof, it's your responsibility; and you can always delegate work, but you can't delegate responsibility.

Ownership requires leadership. When you own something, you have power and authority over it. When you don't own it, you can't do much with it. That's why it's important to own your problems. In order to step into your significance, you must take ownership of the issues in your life. Leaving and denying them will get you nowhere. It will only leave you feeling powerless and like a failure. Take ownership so you can step into authority.

The fifth hidden truth is that the centurion understood the concept of authority. Just as he commanded his men to come, go or carry out an order, so sickness and disease had to obey the word of Jesus. That's why he instructed his friends to go tell Jesus that He didn't have to come; he believed that the authority of His word alone would heal his servant.

Just as Joshua exercised commanding faith when he ordered the sun and moon to stand still (see Joshua 10:12–13), so the centurion exercised commanding faith when he directed Jesus to speak the word on behalf of his servant. In both instances, commanding faith produced the desired results; however, the difference between the two stories is this: the centurion understood the *authority* that Jesus walked in on Earth.

## SIGNIFICANCE COMES FROM AUTHORITY

Jesus said, *"All authority has been given to Me in heaven and on earth"* (Matthew 28:18). He also told His followers, *"Behold, I give you the authority to trample on serpents and scorpions, and over all the power of the enemy"* (Luke 10:19). Notice Jesus didn't give us *power* over the enemy, otherwise we'd be engaged in a never-ending physical battle with him to see who is stronger. Jesus gave us something far better than sheer power; he gave us His authority!

Our significance doesn't come from our power; rather it comes from His authority. Remember the words the Lord spoke to Zerubbabel, who had put his hand to the task of rebuilding the temple: "... *'Not by might nor by power, but by My Spirit,' says the Lord of hosts"* (Zechariah 4:6). We need to keep these words in mind as we carry out the significant work God has given each of us. Our significance, our value and our worth do not come from how powerful or talented we may think we are; our significance comes from the authority of Jesus Christ and His authority, which we walk under.

Once I understood that I walked under the authority of Jesus Christ, I began to speak boldly in the authority of His name. I didn't have to have everything all figured out, and I didn't need to have hundreds of Bible verses committed to memory. I understood that walking in faith in the authority of Jesus Christ was where true power came from.

Jesus understood His authority; therefore, He wasn't concerned about breaking man-made rules. In Jesus' day, the Jews were under oppressive Roman rule and wanted to be free from it. A Jew certainly didn't go to the home of Roman officials for any reason, but Jesus wasn't concerned about breaking man-made rules despite the fact that the centurion had told Him not to come, rather to speak the word.

Jesus was especially adept at breaking the religious rules of the day. Lepers were not to be touched, yet when Jesus touched the man, he was healed. He was called out by the indignant ruler of the synagogue for healing a woman on the Sabbath, and by the religious Pharisees for feeding His disciples on the Sabbath. When asked why He was doing the very things deemed unlawful on the Sabbath, Jesus answered and said, *"The Son of Man is also Lord of the Sabbath"* (Luke 6:5). When we make Jesus Lord of our lives and learn to walk in His authority, the impossible becomes possible.

When I announced that God wanted us to establish a charismatic church in Flagstaff, Arizona, plenty of people were quick to say, "You can't do that, Landon." But we did it. They said, "A church like that will never grow." But it did. When we announced we would launch our own prison ministry with a vision to change our state, they said, "It won't work." But then we saw more than 500 men give their lives to the Lord and, so far, 150 of them have been baptized. In the face of those who declared, "There's no way you're going to be able to afford a bigger building," God gave us a building that was three times the size of the one we used to be in—and it's debt free! And I know that more is on the way—more salvations, baptisms, souls, miracles, signs, wonders, buildings, property and more! God isn't finished yet!

Why does God continually do the seemingly impossible for us? It's because we choose to operate in commanding faith according to Job 22:28, which says, *You shall also decide and decree a thing, and it shall be established for you; and the light [of God's favor] shall shine upon your ways* (AMPC). God continues to shine His favor on us because our commanding faith says, "I don't care what the man-made and religious rules are. I don't care what culture says. I know what my God can do, and my God can do anything!"

I dare you to begin to feel that power of declaring with authority over your own life and the things around you. Speak with bold authority and faith. Don't let your faith die in the silence of intentions; let it grow with every word that comes out of you! Authority has a look and a sound just like winning. If you were observing two different families in their respective homes watching their favorite teams play on TV, I guarantee that you would be able to tell whose team is winning and whose team is losing just by seeing the expression on their faces, and of course hearing them, too. Because winning and losing have a sound and a look, and so does authority. Someone who walks in authority has a look and a sound. I want to tell you, God came to give you exactly what you need, that He is strong in you, and that He wants to make your natural supernatural! Step out of the shadows and into your authority that He has given you.

## COMMANDING FAITH

Astronomy is a natural science that studies everything in the universe beyond Earth's atmosphere, including the sun, moon, other planets, and the stars. Although I never had an interest in studying astronomy, I know, of course, that the sun doesn't revolve around Earth; rather, Earth revolves around the sun, and the moon revolves around Earth. But nobody in Joshua's day knew this.

So, when Joshua spoke to the sun and moon with commanding faith, saying, *"Sun, stand still over Gibeon; and Moon, in the Valley of Aijalon"* (Joshua 10:12), he had no idea that what he asked was, in essence, for God to break His natural rules. I can imagine God thinking, *Joshua, that's not how it works, but I don't care. I'm going to grant your request because of your commanding faith.* And that's exactly what God did.

Remember, we learned that *faith is the substance of things hoped for, the evidence of things not seen* (Hebrews 11:1). God hears our faith even when we don't know what to ask for or how to ask for it, or if we don't yet know the Scripture and how to stand on His Word. God knows what we need, and He wants to meet our needs.

Joshua was ignorant of the natural order of the sun and moon, and how Earth related to each of them, yet in his ignorance he spoke words of commanding faith. To be *ignorant* isn't a bad thing as some suppose; rather, it simply means "lacking in knowledge or information as to a particular subject or fact." I've known people who find their significance in their IQ, but it's not our intelligence that determines our significance. Our significance comes from God, and we demonstrate that significance when we walk in the authority of Jesus. It doesn't matter whether we have a GED or a PhD—God loves and values each one of us equally. He sees our hearts and our faith—though we may yet be ignorant of the way things work in the realm of the Spirit.

Now this is where my faith increases and my significance can have its chance to thrive because I wasn't exactly an A+ student growing up. When I was younger, I blew off my finger with a firecracker. I had a cast on my left hand for months. As a lefty, that affected my performance in school. All my writing and anything to do with my left hand—which now had to be done with my right hand—suffered. My teacher wanted to hold me back because she thought I wasn't smart enough to move on, but that's where my "power mom" came in and made sure her little boy kept moving forward and wasn't held back. When I got into high school, I had to take geometry twice, was pretty much a C+ student and sometimes a B student. After barely graduating through an online homeschool program, I began to realize school wasn't easy for me (slow learner, I know). But I went to Bible college, and the reports and memorization in my first year were very difficult. My friends took hours to complete something that took me days, but I persevered, kept trying, and eventually graduated. I wasn't at the top of my class, but God never left my side and never failed me.

You don't need to be the valedictorian for God to use you in a powerful way. You don't have to know it all for Him to work it all. God will work all things for your good, not because you know it all but because He gave it all—He gave it all on the cross and loves you fiercely. That love will empower you to have commanding faith and move mountains in your life. It will give you the confidence to know you are significant, valuable and important to God! Now people look to me for wisdom, insight, inspiration and a deeper understanding to God and His Word.

But it's not because of how smart I am; it's because I know who is with me, and God gives wisdom to those who ask, without finding fault! (see James 1). When you step out in that place of great faith, He will give you the words to speak and the steps to take. Since I've been walking in my significance, I have received revelation beyond my ability, wisdom beyond my years, favor beyond my faith, and blessings beyond what I deserve! Step into your significance by stepping over your excuses, and speak with commanding faith.

God wants to empower us and get us to the place where we are confident in our commanding faith, but when we go before Him arrogantly, thinking we have every aspect of our lives together, He can't work on us. God can't do a perfect work on someone who thinks they don't need work—that they're already perfect.

It is only when we acknowledge that we need His help that He can do His best work, for the Bible says, *The fear of the* LORD *is instruction in wisdom, and humility comes before honor* (Proverbs 15:33, ESV). Long after he had commanded the sun and moon to stand still, and older and wiser Joshua said, *Now therefore, fear the* LORD, *serve Him in sincerity and in truth ...* (Joshua 24:14). When we go before God with humility and a sincere heart—complete with all our faults and blemishes—and ask Him to teach us His ways, He will answer that prayer in ways we could never imagine.

Now in Joshua's story, there is a key principle regarding commanding faith. Joshua didn't go to God about his problem; rather, he went to his problem with his God, and he began to speak to his situation. Far too many of us unknowingly delay the answers to our prayers because we spend all our prayer time talking to God about our problems. "Did you see what they did to me at work, Lord?" "I just don't know how I'm going to make my mortgage payment this month." "Well, I guess you must be trying to teach me something through this sickness I've been enduring."

Instead of talking to God *about* our problems, we are to *speak* to our problems with commanding faith about our God! Tell cancer, "My God is the God who heals!" Tell addiction, "My God is the God who delivers"; tell the enemy that has your family, "My God is the God who saves." It doesn't say when you have faith in God you can say, "God, please move that mountain." The Bible says when you have faith, you can speak, "Mountain, move," and it will be cast into the sea (see Mark 11:23). Stop introducing God to all your issues and start introducing all your problems to God! Speak with commanding faith!

Commanding faith walks and speaks in the authority of Jesus Christ, who said, "... *In the world you will have tribulation; but be of good cheer, I have overcome the world*" (John 16:33). He also said, "*Therefore I say to you, whatever things you ask when you pray, believe that you receive them, and you will have them*" (Mark 11:24).

I believe God is telling us, "If you'll simply stop the difficult process of trying to work out your problems in your own strength and wisdom, and instead turn to face your problems, bringing Me to the problem, you'll find that victory will quickly come."

## THE VICTORY IS YOURS

The situation did not look good as Joshua and the mighty men of valor prepared for war. Surrounded by the armies from five nations, they were significantly outnumbered. But God was with Joshua; therefore, he and his men were in the majority. That's when God said, *"Do not fear them, for I have delivered them into your hand; not a man of them shall stand before you"* (Joshua 10:8).

In other words, God said, "Joshua, today you are going to have the victory. If you take Me to your enemies, I'll give them into your hand." Joshua *knew* he and his men would win the battle, so he went out and commanded the sun and moon, saying, "You've got to stand still because my God wants me to have the victory." As Joshua spoke to his circumstances about his God, his God's Word and his God's will, the entire solar system stopped so that he could experience God's promised victory. The whole solar system! Now that's powerful commanding faith! Joshua was saying, "I'm too important to God for you not to listen to me. I'm too significant and my mission is too vital—the sun, moon, stars and planets must listen to what I say because God has me on a mission! My victory means too much."

This is how we should see ourselves, but too many of us discount our value and water down the level of importance to our mission, purpose and self-worth. I think that we just chalk it up to that God doesn't want us to win all the time, or it's not so important to be victorious. But when we discount our value, we discredit His grace! Your value comes from Him and His purpose in your life! Don't water down your value or lower the importance of your purpose. You are a child of God and what you do on earth will echo for eternity! It's hard to be victorious when it's easier to play the victim, but the Bible says we are more than conquerors (see Romans 8:37), and we are victorious in Christ Jesus! Decide to not play the victim because you are meant to win—and yes, it's important to God that you win!

Throughout the Bible we see that God's plan for His people has always been victory; however, as New Testament believers, we have a new and better covenant with God through Jesus Christ. The Bible says, *But now He has obtained a more excellent ministry, inasmuch as He is also Mediator of a better covenant, which was established on better promises* (Hebrews 8:6).

The apostle Paul wrote these words to the believers in Corinth: *But thanks be to God, who gives us the victory through our Lord Jesus Christ* (1 Corinthians 15:57). And John said, *For whatever is born of God overcomes the world. And this is the victory that has overcome the world—our faith* (1 John 5:4). God wants us to have victory over our enemies, over our adversaries, over those who hate us. But to achieve that victory, it's important to understand this powerful truth: *For we do not wrestle against flesh and blood, but against principalities, against powers, against the rulers of the darkness of this age, against spiritual hosts of wickedness in the heavenly places* (Ephesians 6:12). In other words, instead of dealing with the people who stand against us, we are instead to deal with the spirit that influences the people behind the attack.

Those under the influence of a spirit who want to vex and destroy us are not coming against us only, they're also coming against God. In God's love for humankind, He will always create a reconciliation moment for each person, saying, "You need to humble yourself." They will have to come to terms with who God is in their lives, and they will have to repent. *The Lord is ... not willing that any should perish but that all should come to repentance* (2 Peter 3:9).

It is not only the unsaved who need to repent. Oftentimes, believers can unknowingly align with the wrong side of their assignment. That's why it's so important to live a life of repentance because that's what will refresh and reset ourselves, ensuring we are on the right side and the right page with what God is trying to do. A repentant lifestyle keeps God in in the center of our lives and situations we face.

When we bring God into our situation—using our authority in Jesus Christ to speak with commanding faith to the spiritual forces that try to seek to steal, kill, and destroy— those forces must bow their knee to the name of Jesus (see John 10:10 and Ephesians 6:12). Anytime someone comes against us with another argument, problem or issue, we can point them right back to Jesus. Remember that Snickers® candy bar commercial about being "hangry" and just not acting like yourself? After you eat a Snickers, you're good.

Well, that's exactly how to handle people who come at you in an offensive or defensive way; you know they aren't themselves, but that it's a spiritual thing. Point them back to Jesus by letting them know they need to go spend some time with Him to "satisfy their hunger!" If they don't know God, our commanding faith can open the door for them to meet Jesus. Commanding faith enables us to stand in the middle of the battlefield and cause the forces of darkness to stand still so that God can deliver the victory.

We won't be able to beat the enemy if we are constantly fighting each other. We don't even have time to be fighting, and we shouldn't be getting beat by the enemy. God wants us to win. When Jesus comes, He doesn't want to find a defeated body of Christ, wearing tattered garments and all hunched over, declaring, "We survived!" No! He wants a glorious and beautiful bride wearing spotless garments and shining with the light of His love.

Perhaps you're saying, "That all sounds real good, but I've been so belittled and devalued that it's hard for me to get comfortable with the idea of being significant and speaking with authority." Believe me—I get it. I've been in churches where some pastors twist the Scripture to make people believe in their unworthiness. For instance, they quote Isaiah 64:6: *But we are all like an unclean thing, and all our righteousness are like filthy rags …*; but they fail to quote the New Testament truth that *He made Him who knew no sin to be sin for us, that we might become the righteousness of God in Him* (2 Corinthians 5:21).

When you live a defeated lifestyle that doesn't include exercising commanding faith, everything around you withers and fades, bringing about a loss of hope. You live life as a victim rather than the victor God created you to be. This is the reason it is so important that you understand the depth of God's love for you, and how significant you are to His plan for humankind in this day and hour. He doesn't care how much you know or what titles you may have earned. He wants you to be bold and exercise the commanding faith that comes from your authority in Jesus Christ.

Be the James Bond, the Wonder Woman, the centurion, the Joshua in your story. You know what it looks like in the natural, and now you know what it can look like in the supernatural. And it's all for you right now.

When you can see who Jesus is in your life, you'll see the authority that is yours through His sacrifice on the cross. It doesn't matter how unworthy you may *feel*; all you must do to walk in His authority is simply *receive* it. You may need to start out taking baby steps, but as you become more confident in His authority, you'll begin to walk differently, talk differently and live differently. Suddenly, your significance will come to life and shine brightly. Relationships will be healed, and your finances will turn around. You will see your faith come to fruition because God says, "Okay, I'm in this with you. Use your commanding faith to speak to the mountain that stands before you, and then watch and see what I will do in your behalf."

Take a moment to say this prayer out loud:

*Father, I receive Your word about commanding faith, and I choose at this moment to walk in it and declare it. I declare an outpouring of Your Spirit over my city, my state, and my nation. I command peace and prosperity over my home and my family.*

*I now speak to principalities, powers, rulers of darkness of this age, and spiritual wickedness in high places, and I command you to cease your activity against me and my assignment by using people to discourage and withstand me. In the name and authority of Jesus Christ, I command those people under your influence to come to repentance and be set free.*

*I choose to walk in the authority of Jesus Christ. This is my winning season, my season to prosper in my business, my family, and my health. I thank You, Father, that You want me to overcome and that You will help me vanquish the enemies that try to come against me, for they are not just coming against me, but they also are coming against You.*

*I use my commanding faith to declare that not only is my life significant, but my assignment is also significant. Though it may seem impossible, I will complete it because with You, all things are possible. So, thank You, Lord, for pouring out Your power in my life that all who see it may give glory to You.*

## SIGNIFICANT APPLICATION

**1.** Name a time you had a commanding presence or moment.

_____

_____

_____

_____

**2.** Name one time you had a "I wish I had said ..." moment.

_____

_____

_____

_____

**3.** Make a list of 7 positive and praiseworthy things that have been said about you.

_____

_____

_____

_____

**4.** Write about a time that you were generous and saw generosity come back to you.

_____

_____

_____

_____

**5.** *What problem or situation have you been taking to God? "Flip the script" and instead take God to your problem.*

_____

_____

_____

_____

**6.** *What excuse has been holding you back from stepping into commanding faith?*

_____

_____

_____

_____

**7.** *What's one way you can start taking more authority in your home?*

_____

_____

_____

_____

# CHAPTER EIGHT

# YOU SHALL RECEIVE POWER

‖

I hope each chapter of this book so far has helped unlock a new area of defining and directing your value and significance. Any opportunity you get to help create a moment that frees you will soon become a momentum that carries you. It's the snowball effect. It may start small, but as it keeps rolling, it will get larger. So, push that same snowball down a hill and watch it get larger with momentum. Moments of freedom and empowerment in your life are just like that. They will build on each other, and if you keep moving forward, pretty soon, it becomes a movement that will carry you in life!

Remember, it's difficult to walk with confidence, authority, and boldness without power; and if you have no power, you feel weak. If you feel weak, you feel insignificant. It would be terrible for Christ to pay the price so that you could be free, saved and redeemed only to leave you powerless and unable to walk with the confidence of knowing who you are and what you are capable of. It would feel so impossible if Jesus just said to go make disciples, baptize and teach them—change the world … and nothing else (see Matthew 28:19–20). But before He was taken up to Heaven, He gave this reassurance *"… you shall receive power when the Holy Spirit has come upon you; and you shall be witnesses to Me in Jerusalem, and in all Judea and Samaria, and to the end of the earth"* (Acts 1:8).

We learned in Chapter 3 that each of us has an assignment from God, and that our individual assignments are every bit as significant as we are. Whether we are in full-time ministry, running a business, working in retail or homeschooling the next generation, all assignments are significant. It is in our assigned work that we carry out our *calling* to take the Gospel into all the world. However, it is not possible for us to carry out our calling within our assigned work without power from God.

I often wonder what the disciples must have thought when the risen Jesus spoke those words from Matthew 28. Of course, they understood what it was to heal the sick and cast out demons, for they'd seen Jesus do those very things. But what did Jesus mean about speaking with new tongues? And what about going into all the world? (see Mark 16:15–17). Remember in that day, nobody yet knew the world was round, much less how to get to every place and person to preach the Gospel. To further complicate the matter, the only way to travel was either on foot or on the back of an animal.

Jesus knew all of this. He also knew the disciples could not fulfill His mandate in their own strength. You've probably heard the phrase "God doesn't call the equipped; He equips the called." When God called you into this brand-new life of freedom, grace and significance, He also was ready to equip you and empower you for every good work.

## SMALL BUT SIGNIFICANT

As you now know, I was called to ministry at a young age, had a few accidents and wasn't the strongest student in school. Add to that list (as if it wasn't enough), when I was 15, I entered high school standing at a "commanding" 5′3″ weighing in at 85lbs! I attended American Heritage Academy in Carrollton, Texas—a young school, but it was a strong athletic one in a suburb of Dallas/Fort Worth where sports is everything! I was terrified! Since it was a smaller private school, it had junior high, and elementary on the same campus. So when I walked through the halls of my new high school, I was greeted by some older high school girls who automatically looked excited to see me. They welcomed me with open arms, saying how cute I was, and how precious I was—all the things a young man going through puberty does not want to hear! As they assaulted me with a barrage of insults only fitting for a tiny puppy, they began to tell me that the junior high was the other way.

I quickly spoke up in the deepest tone I could muster and said, "Say girl, get off me—I'm in high school!" As I walked away, I mumbled "They weren't that cute anyway!" What a way to start high school that was! I quickly joined some teams and gave it my best shot. I actually got on the football team but not exactly as starter. My coach made me the captain of the submarine, which meant during a game if he needed a sub to go in, I was the guy to go get the sub and send him in. Because I was so small, I didn't really play much unless we were way ahead in the fourth quarter, and because of my size I quickly developed a nickname "Pee wee"! It actually caught on, and some of the fans, including parents, actually made signs so that when we were winning—which was pretty often—they would pull out the signs and chant "Pee wee, Pee wee, Pee wee!" That meant that it was time to put the star into the game—yes, yours truly.

Now just because I had practiced, suited up, and worked hard to be able to play didn't mean I was not terrified to go into a game. I remember one time I got put into the game, and a running back came plowing my direction as if he were looking for me. If you don't know football, that's not normal for an offensive player to seek out a defensive player like that. He came running at me, and I just wanted to survive. So I kind of fell/ducked as he came at me causing him to flip over me and inadvertently get "tackled" by me. When I came up, all I knew was I survived, and he was down. We ended up winning that game of course, and I like to think it was because of me. At least that's the way I like to remember it.

There was a young man in the Bible that I can completely relate to, and his name was Gideon. He was a small guy and came from what he considered to be an insignificant family. God called him to do something great with his life, but he only felt powerless and too insignificant to do so.

In Judges 6:11–16, we learn about Gideon. He considered himself the least and disqualified himself before even trying to do what God was asking of him. God asked him to help set the people free from the Midianites—to tear down idols and help the people of God turn their hearts and worship back to Him and live in the freedom He desired for them. Now Gideon eventually did what the Lord asked after testing God and God testing Gideon; and after Gideon won over the

Midianites with the Lord, it was a victory of peace that lasted for 40 years.

Forty years represents a generation, which means a whole generation knew peace because of Gideon. I wonder if we can win this battle of finding our own true significance, how many generations would know peace and freedom in their lives? Because this journey you've been on may have felt like it's just about you, but let me tell you: It's about the generation after you—your kids, grandkids and great-grandkids. It's time we start winning some of these important battles so that the generations after us can walk in a greater place because of us.

The battle isn't just about you; it's about who's coming after you. Part of your significant life is that more people of value and importance will come after you, through you and impacted by you in one way or another. Never let the enemy try to get you to think his fight is only with you; it's with everyone who will ever be impacted by you. That's why the Bible says a three-strand cord is not easily broken (see Ecclesiastes 4:12); it speaks to generational strength, which the Scripture repeats over and over again ... "I am the God of Abraham, Isaac, and Jacob." Generational significance is more important than we can truly understand. No matter what you are going through, just remember it's more than just about you—more than you by yourself. Pastor Kevin Gerald, in his book *Naked and Unafraid*, talks about this and encourages people to "think 3"—think of three generations any time you are doing anything. I believe this is one of the things that motivated Gideon.

Initially, when God showed up (Judges 6:11), Gideon was hiding in a winepress, threshing wheat. I wonder how many believers—because of fear and insecurity—have been hiding from everyone else, afraid to see what they are really capable of? Because the moment the Angel of the Lord saw Gideon and called him out of hiding, He spoke to the champion in him, saying, "You mighty man of valor"; or, "You mighty warrior!" The Lord didn't rebuke him for hiding, make fun of him or ridicule him. God wanted to call out the champion in him not the coward. Many times, I truly think that a lot of us who battle fear, insecurities, and doubts think that when God shows up or sees us, He's going to be mad, disappointed or at least slightly irritated with us—like we're not all He hoped for. But that's not the case at all! When God shows up and sees we've been hiding, He doesn't call us out—He calls us up!

Now let's see what happened in the book of Acts as the disciples and a group of followers, including Mary the mother of Jesus, when they were gathered to pray.

> *When the Day of Pentecost had fully come, they were all with one accord in one place. And suddenly there came a sound from heaven, as of a rushing mighty wind, and it filled the whole house where they were sitting. Then there appeared to them divided tongues, as of fire, and one sat upon each of them. And they were all filled with the Holy Spirit and began to speak with other tongues, as the Spirit gave them utterance.* (ACTS 2:1-4)

We learned in Chapter 2 that each time we read a Bible story we need to ask ourselves three questions: Who is speaking? Who are they speaking to? And what did they know that we don't know? This story speaks of the Day of Pentecost, an annual event the Jews knew as Shavuot (shav-oo-oat), or the Feast of Weeks. The starting point of this celebration began 50 days from the day Passover ended. The literal meaning of the Greek word *pentecost* is "50."

That group of believers had gathered with a clear purpose per Jesus' instructions to "*tarry in the city of Jerusalem until you are endued with power from on high*" (Luke 24:49). They had no idea how long they were to wait for something they may well have thought was taking forever. But the Bible says that *suddenly* there came a sound and a wind that filled the whole house, accompanied by tongues of fire as those who had gathered in unity were filled with the Holy Spirit and began to speak in tongues. In just a moment of time God moved supernaturally, enduing those believers with power from on high, and the Church was born. The Bible describes what happened next, after the believers spilled into the streets.

> *And there were dwelling in Jerusalem Jews, devout men, from every nation under heaven. And when this sound occurred, the multitude came together, and were confused, because everyone heard them speak in his own language. Then they were all amazed and marveled, saying to one another, "Look, are not all these who speak Galileans? And how is it that we hear, each in our own language in which we were born? ... we hear them speaking in our own tongues the wonderful works of*

*God." So they were all amazed and perplexed, saying
to one another, "Whatever could this mean?" Others
mocking said, "They are full of new wine."* (ACTS 2:5-13)

When the supernatural move of God spilled over from
where the believers had gathered to pray into the public places
where devout Jews from other nations had come to celebrate
the Feast of Weeks—Pentecost—people were astounded by
what they saw and heard.

When the people asked, "Are not all these who speak
Galileans?" they were pointing out that there was no way
those speaking could do so in so many different languages.
Some people mocked the believers, saying they must be
drunk. I personally believe that experience of being ridiculed
only caused faith to arise, for the next thing we see is Peter
speaking to the crowd.

*But Peter, standing up with the eleven, raised his
voice and said to them, "Men of Judea and all who dwell
in Jerusalem, let this be known to you, and heed my
words. For these are not drunk, as you suppose, since it
is only the third hour of the day. But this is what was
spoken by the prophet Joel: 'And it shall come to pass
in the last days, says God, that I will pour out of My
Spirit on all flesh; your sons and your daughters shall
prophesy, your young men shall see visions, your old men
shall dream dreams. and on My menservants and on My
maidservants I will pour out My Spirit in those days; and
they shall prophesy.'"* (ACTS 2:14-18)

Peter, who only 50 days earlier had denied knowing Jesus three times, now boldly proclaimed the Gospel. What had changed? Peter had received the power Jesus had spoken about; the Holy Spirit had come upon him. This was a moment of provocation for Peter, pushing him into his destiny—into his significant purpose.

> *Then Peter said to them, "Repent, and let every one of you be baptized in the name of Jesus Christ for the remission of sins; and you shall receive the gift of the Holy Spirit. For the promise is to you and to your children, and to all who are afar off, as many as the Lord will call."*
>
> *And with many other words he testified and exhorted them, saying, "Be saved from this perverse generation." Then those who gladly received his word were baptized; and that day about three thousand souls were added to them.* (ACTS 2:38-41)

Notice the final sentence speaks of those who *gladly* received Peter's word. As a pastor, I know the importance of believers being glad, or happy, of choosing to smile more each day. There's no reason for us to be sad. Some may say, "Oh, but don't understand the problems I have to deal with." True, but then we all have problems to deal with. Here's what I've learned about problems: When we think about our problems and talk about them, we literally magnify them.

Instead of magnifying our problems, we should magnify God. Don't enlarge your problem, because then those problems will always seem too large. When you magnify God, that's when God becomes bigger than any problem. Challenge your-self to not only see God but see the good around you, because when you start seeing the good, you'll start seeing God.

We have reason to be happy, to rejoice, to celebrate and to magnify God. The Bible says we've been given *the oil of joy for mourning, the garment of praise for the spirit of heaviness ...* (Isaiah 61:3).

Let's get happy! Smile!

## GOD'S POWER WITHIN US

I want us to look again at the words of Jesus in Acts 1:8: *"But you shall receive power when the Holy Spirit has come upon you ..."* The Greek word translated as *power* in this verse is *dunamis,* from which we get the English word *dynamite.* The power Jesus referred to can be described as "explosive power" or "the fire of God." This is the kind of power that dwells in us when the Holy Spirit comes upon us.

Another thing I want to point out about Acts 1:8 is the term "the Holy Spirit." The Holy Spirit is not a name; rather, it is a title given to the third person of the Godhead. The Holy Spirit is not an "it"—the Holy Spirit is God Himself. Some believers who do not yet understand this truth think the Holy Spirit is weird. But there's nothing weird about the power of God dwelling within us.

Some church denominations teach that the miracles, signs and wonders of the Holy Spirit were meant only for those liv-ing in Bible days, and that they no longer exist. But this is not true. We just read Peter's words in Acts 2:38–39: *For the prom-ise is to you and to your children, and to all who are afar off, as many as the Lord our God will call.* God Himself said, *"For I am the* L*ord, I do not change"* (Malachi 3:6); and He is described by James as *the Father of lights, with whom there is no variation or shadow of turning* (James 1:17).

In other words, the promises of God have no expiration date. Times may change, people may change, and circumstances may change, but God does not change. The same God who poured out His Spirit on people for moments, times, and seasons in the Old Testament is the same God who poured out His Spirit on believers in the New Testament.

Jesus *chose* to go to the cross and die for us. His sacrifice is what enabled us to receive the power of the Holy Spirit from God, because Jesus knew we would need it to accomplish all we are called to do and to live the significant, victorious life He has prepared for each of us. To live for Christ through the power of God is intended to bring passion to our lives, yet many people feel weak, powerless, and without zeal. That is not how God wants us to experience life. When we feel powerful, we can live passionately; we can step out with confidence and excitement because we know we aren't going to lose. We have the explosive fire of God within us.

Sadly, many believers choose to receive the Lamb of God, Jesus, as their Savior and Lord; but they don't want to receive the power of the Holy Spirit. God never intended believers to live without the fire of God within them. Nowhere in the Bible do we see this truth more vividly illustrated than in the Feast of Passover.

Considered the foundational holiday for the nation of Israel, Passover marks the deliverance of Israel from Egypt.

The original Passover was held on the night of the Exodus, when God instructed every Israelite household in Egypt to choose a lamb without blemish, sacrifice it, and mark the doorposts and lintel of each house where they lived with its blood. Later that night, when God passed through Egypt to strike the firstborn of every household, He would see the blood on the Israelites' doorposts and pass over those houses. In the meantime, the Israelites were to subsequently eat the slain lamb as their Passover meal (see Exodus 12:1–11).

We understand that Jesus is the fulfillment of the Passover festival. John the Baptist first identified Him as the Messiah, saying, *"Behold! The Lamb of God who takes away the sin of the world!"* (John 1:29). And the apostle Paul said, *for indeed Christ, our Passover, was sacrificed for us* (1 Corinthians 5:7).

When God instituted the Passover meal, He said, *"Then they shall eat the flesh on that night; roasted in fire, with unleavened bread and with bitter herbs they shall eat it. Do not eat it raw, nor boiled at all with water, but roasted in fire—its head with its legs and its entrails"* (Exodus 12:8–9). In other words, God was saying, "Take the lamb, but do not put it in a pot or a pan. Put it right in the fire because you can't get the lamb without the fire."

Jesus Christ is *our* Passover Lamb of God, and the Holy Spirit is the fire. When we get saved, we also get the fire of God because the Lamb and the fire are not separate. When we make Jesus Christ Savior and Lord, we have access to the Holy Spirit and the power of God that has been poured out on us.

## POSITIONING DETERMINES OUTPOURING

Prior to His crucifixion, Jesus instructed His disciples to wait in Jerusalem until they were endued with power from on high. He knew that being in the right position was critical to their receiving the promised outpouring of the power of God. When we, the body of Christ, position ourselves correctly, God will pour out His blessing, favor, increase, miracles, signs and wonders. He will pour out an experience that will transform our lives; however, He will not do it while we are still dysfunctional.

When I say we need to be in the right position, I'm not talking about literally being in Jerusalem. The believers who had gathered in Jerusalem to pray were in a position of unity, for the Bible says, *When the Day of Pentecost had fully come, they were all with one accord in one place* (Acts 2:1). When I think of being in one accord with other believers, I'm reminded what it is to sing in harmony: though multiple people sing different notes, those notes compose one beautiful, main melody of a single song.

If we want to experience an outpouring of God's power, we must first position ourselves in unity with other believers. We mustn't take part in anything that divides the body of Christ, criticizing the beliefs of another denomination or ridiculing someone because they interpret the Scripture differently than we do. If we don't agree with a particular television preacher, instead of berating him or her, we can simply turn off the TV! Paul dealt with similar issues within the body of Christ in his day, particularly between his followers and those who followed Apollos:

*... For as long as [there are] envying and jealousy and wrangling and factions among you, are you not unspiritual and of the flesh, behaving yourselves after a human standard and like mere (unchanged) men?*

*For when one says, I belong to Paul, and another, I belong to Apollos, are you not [proving yourselves] ordinary (unchanged) men?*

*What then is Apollos? What is Paul? Ministering servants [not heads of parties] through whom you believed, even as the Lord appointed to each his task ...*

*For we are fellow workmen (joint promoters, laborers together) with and for God ....*

(1 CORINTHIANS 3:3–5, 9, AMPC)

Paul was saying, it's not whose church you go to or preacher you like that's important; it's the mission of God we all have in common that's significant.

In addition to being in unity with others in the body of Christ, we must have a sense of expectancy that God will do something great for us. I always prepare my Sunday sermon ahead of time, and then arrive at church *expecting* the presence of the Holy Spirit and an outpouring of His power.

Far too many believers, however, choose to live in the doldrums of doubt, discouragement, and disbelief because they don't expect to see God's promises fulfilled in their lives. Instead of declaring, "I can do all things through Christ who strengthens me," they start every sentence with "I can't." They may read a promise of God, and yet speak words of doubt about that promise, saying, "I don't know about that," or "Can we *really* expect that from God?" They are like those believers described in the book of Hebrews: *For indeed the gospel was preached to us as well as to them; but the word which they heard did not profit them, not being mixed with faith in those who heard it"* (Hebrews 4:2). Part of discovering your significance is choosing to not be deceived with doubt but deciding to believe that His promises are for you personally.

Now, if God had never fulfilled any of His promises in your life, or in the life of other believers, if He'd never healed anyone of cancer or delivered anyone from an addiction or depression, we would all be living in a very dark place. We could say, "Well it's never been done" or "That's impossible— I've never heard of that." But the Bible says, *For all the promises of God in Him are Yes, and in Him Amen ...* (2 Corinthians 1:20); and *He has delivered us from the power of darkness and conveyed us into the kingdom of the Son of His love* (Colossians 1:13).

The *Amplified Bible* (classic edition) says, *For with God nothing is ever impossible and no word from God shall be without power or impossible of fulfillment* (Luke 1:37).

And the truth is that God has done it; Jesus has done it. And if He's done it before, He can do it again. He can do it for you!

I want you to think about a specific promise of God that you want to see fulfilled in your life. Perhaps you or someone you know has told you it can't be done, but I'm here to tell you it *can* be done, and it *will* be done! Because our Father who is in heaven, hallowed is His name. His kingdom has come, and His will is done on the earth as it is in heaven (see Matthew 6:10).

In heaven there is no sickness, lack, addiction or depression. So, when you're battling anything that does not exist in heaven, take authority over it in the name of Jesus and say, "Oh no, no, no! Jesus Christ has already delivered me, and whom the Son has set free is free indeed!" If someone says you can't be filled with the Holy Spirit and that the miracles of Bible days have passed away, don't believe them. People are still being filled with the Holy Spirit, giants are still being slain, and miracles, signs and wonders are still manifesting all over the earth.

The Bible describes Jesus going throughout the land preaching, teaching, and healing every manner of sickness and disease, yet Jesus told His disciples, *"Most assuredly, I say to you, he who believes in Me, the works that I do he will also do; and greater works than these he will do, because I go to My Father"* (John 14:12). We see this very thing happen on a consistent basis at our church in Flagstaff.

For instance, my father recently came and preached the Sunday morning message to our congregation. As he was preaching, he received a word of knowledge that God was going to heal the leg of someone in attendance. My father stopped and delivered that word, and then he finished his message. We found out later what had happened.

A family who attends regularly brought another family with them that morning. One of the guests, a man, particularly didn't want to be there because he'd been dealing with a painful leg issue for about six months. Following the service, he sent this text to the family that had invited him: "I don't know what happened at church today, but when the pastor spoke that word about a leg being healed, something changed. I left church this morning with no pain for the first time in six months. I am totally healed, and everything is good. I'll definitely be back!"

Someone may say, "Oh, that healing stuff is a third-world country thing," or "I bet they just made that up—it didn't really happen." Just because someone hasn't personally witnessed a miracle doesn't mean it isn't real. We must never allow doubt to rule our lives. Oftentimes the very area in which the enemy is trying to hold us captive is directly related to the assignment from heaven for which God has anointed us.

For instance, the enemy tried to hold Peter captive so that he would not preach the Gospel. I can just imagine on the night Jesus was arrested Satan whispering in Peter's ear, "Peter, they're going to arrest you too, so just deny that you know Jesus." And we know that's exactly what Peter did; however, once the Holy Spirit came upon him, Peter became a powerful witness for Jesus, and in only one day over 3,000 people were saved. The very area where the enemy tried to hold Peter captive soon became his area of anointing—his significant work assignment as an evangelist.

Perhaps you are now struggling in an area of your own life, and you sense the enemy is trying to destroy you. If so, then it's likely this is the very area of your anointing—your significant work. I know this because it happened to me. The enemy tried to take my voice when I was nine years old, but God miraculously restored my trachea. And today I am preaching the Gospel and seeing God do the miraculous in the lives of believers. God will do whatever it takes for you too so that you can be free to step into your significance and accomplish all He's called you to do.

Make the decision right now to position yourself for an outpouring of God's power in your life. Make it your purpose to be in unity with all in the body of Christ, and live in a state of continual expectancy of the great things God wants to do in your behalf—each and every day. *Expect* the new life He has for you. *Expect* a new level of hope to arise. *Expect* to see all His promises fulfilled in your life!

## A MOMENT OF PROVOCATION

When God's power begins to manifest in your life, you can't remain in the same place; therefore, God will push you toward your significant work. That's exactly what He did on the day of Pentecost. Once those believers had been filled with the Holy Spirit, God pushed them out of the upper room and into the street in a moment of provocation.

Provocation is simply an act that *provokes,* which means "to stir up, arouse, or call forth; to incite or stimulate; to give rise to, induce, or bring about." God wasn't going to allow the moment of the outpouring of His Spirit to become stifled and not become the movement He intended it to be. Likewise, He is not going to allow us to become stifled and bogged down by our own issues and sin when the Bible says, *as His divine power has given us all things that pertain to life and godliness, through the knowledge of Him who called us by glory and virtue* (2 Peter 1:3).

In His great love for us, God is going to say, "Okay, are you done with playing the pity game, with wallowing in your sin and shame? I'm calling you to get up and get going!" God is going to stir us up just enough that we become uncomfortable where we are, and then move us forward into our destinies. That's exactly what happened when (Simon) Peter encountered Jesus for the first time.

> *So it was, as the multitude pressed about [Jesus] to hear the word of God, that He stood by the lake of Gennesaret, and saw two boats standing by the lake; but the fisherman had gone from them and were washing their nets. Then He got into one of the boats, which was Simon's, and asked him to put out a little from the land. And he sat down and taught the multitudes from the boat.*
>
> *When He had stopped speaking, He said to Simon, "Launch out into the deep and let down your nets for a catch."*
>
> *But Simon answered and said to Him, "Master, we have toiled all night and caught nothing; nevertheless at Your word I will let down the net." And when they had done this, they caught a great number of fish, and their net was breaking. So they signaled to their partners in the other boat to come help them. And they came and filled both boats, so that they began to sink. When Simon Peter saw it, he fell down at Jesus' knees, saying, "Depart from me, for I am a sinful man, O Lord!"*
>
> *... And Jesus said to Simon, "Do not be afraid. From now on you will catch men." So when they had brought their boats to land, they forsook all and followed Him.*
>
> (LUKE 5:1–8, 10)

It's interesting that, following Jesus' crucifixion and resurrection, Peter and several other disciples were again fishing when the Lord appeared to them, though at first they did not recognize Him. After they had fished all night and caught nothing, He said to them, *"Cast the net on the right side of the boat, and you will find some." So they cast, and now they were not able to draw it in because of the multitude of fish. Therefore that disciple whom Jesus loved said to Peter, "It is the Lord!"* ... (John 21:6–7).

Here's the point I want you to see in this story: This second encounter between Jesus and Peter in a fishing environment occurred sometime *before* the day of Pentecost, when Peter was endued with the power of the Holy Spirit. Jesus had already called Peter to be a fisher of men and had spent three years with him and the other disciples demonstrating the power of God through miracles, signs, and wonders. Yet Peter had denied Jesus and returned to his nets. You know what this tells me? Peter saved his boat, and he saved his nets; he had a "plan B."

We are oftentimes like Peter in that we too have a plan B when it comes to the call of God on our lives and the significant work He has prepared us for. It's as though we are listening to the enemy's voice as he says, "Is the work God has called you to *really* significant? Is it *really* going to happen? Is God *really* going to heal your marriage? Is going to church, praying, and reading your Bible *really* going to make a difference in your situation?" Even though you may not see the promises of God fulfilled in your life yet, don't give up but persevere to do things God's way because He who promised is faithful (see Hebrews 10:23 and 2 Peter 3:9).

## A MOMENT BECOMES A MOVEMENT

Keeping in mind Peter's journey from called by Jesus to empowered by the Holy Spirit, let's look again at the first verse of Acts 2: *When the Day of Pentecost had fully come, they were all with one accord in one place.* Jesus had told His followers to wait in Jerusalem until they were endued with power from on high. We don't know exactly how many days they gathered to pray in the upper room most say a full 10, but at some point, they had to be thinking, *We're ready. We're in one accord and we have a sense of expectancy. We are in position, so when is this going to happen?* When the Spirit of God rushed into that upper room with power, that group of 120 people became an army. Along with the others, Peter stumbled out into the streets speaking in other tongues before people from other nations who had gathered there.

But then something happened. When the people mocked the believers saying they were drunk, Peter suddenly started walking in his evangelistic assignment as he boldly testified of Jesus and explained Joel's prophecy of the outpouring of the Spirit of God. *Then Peter said to them, "Repent, and let every one of you be baptized in the name of Jesus Christ for the remission of sins; and you shall receive the gift of the Holy Spirit. For the promise is to you and to your children, and to all who are afar off, as many as the Lord our God will call"* (Acts 2:38–39).

And with that, a moment became a movement as the Church—the body of Christ—was born.

All of us have experienced important or symbolic moments in our lives; however, in the natural, these moments merely come and go and then fade to distant memories. But a moment from the Holy Spirit will become a movement in your soul, which has the power to reach a city, a state, a nation, and even the world.

The calling of God for believers to go into the world and preach the Gospel is not limited only to those of us assigned to serve in full-time ministry. You were created to fulfill a calling within your assigned work, whether you run a business, work for someone else, or are at home, raising the next generation. The point is this: Neither you nor I can be successful in our assigned work without the power of the Holy Spirit.

I was blessed to be raised in a home where salvation, water baptism, and the power of the Holy Spirit were the spiritual foundation in my family. I first encountered the power of God for myself at a very young age, after which I routinely experienced dreams and visions. Although I prophesied and prayed in tongues, I was not immune to the devil's efforts to prevent me from walking in my calling to take the Gospel to the world and accepting my assignment to be a preacher. Instead of continuing to surrender to God, I actually ran away from Him. But when I made the adult decision to surrender to Him, I once again experienced the power of the Holy Spirit, praying in tongues on a regular basis.

When we don't know what to pray and we pray in tongues, the Holy Spirit prays *through* us the perfect prayers according to the will of God (see Romans 8:26–27). I didn't understand the power of this kind of praying until I became old enough and wise enough to realize I really didn't know how to pray. I discovered that I *needed* the Holy Spirit to pray through me and for me. Whenever I felt lost, without direction, or concerned for my family, I experienced comfort, power, and direction as I allowed the Holy Spirit to pray God's perfect will through me.

Perhaps you are a new believer, just learning the Word of God, or maybe you were raised in a church environment that didn't acknowledge and teach the power of the Holy Spirit. If you want the power of the Holy Spirit in your life, it is available to you. You are a significant member of the body of Christ, called to take the Gospel into all the world and experience the signs Jesus said would follow His believers (see Mark 16:17–18). This promise isn't only for those in full-time ministry; it is for *all* believers, for all time.

So if you feel small like me and Gideon, or battle insecurities and fears like Peter, the power of your significance comes from the power of the Holy Spirit living in you.

Remember, it was Jesus who baptized those believers in the Holy Spirit on the Day of Pentecost, and He still baptizes believers in the Holy Spirit today. If you want Jesus to baptize you in the Holy Spirit, you can receive His power right now, right where you are. Take a few moments to pray this prayer:

*Jesus, You are the one who baptizes in the Holy Spirit, and I ask you to baptize me, right here and right now. I receive the Holy Spirit and the promised enduement of power from on high.*

*Holy Spirit, set me on fire with the dunamis power of God, the explosive power of God in my life, and bless me with the gifts of the Holy Spirit. I pray this in the name of Jesus. Amen.*

Now begin to say the name of Jesus over and over as you let the Holy Spirit's gift of a new language begin to flow from your lips. Receiving His gift of this new language is as simple as allowing your tongue and mouth to move in a way that forms words in a language that you do not know.

I believe this moment of empowerment will become a movement in your life as God propels you into the significant assignment that has been prepared just for you, in which you—along with millions of others in the body of Christ—fulfill Jesus' commission to take the Gospel into all the world. Always remember this: *You are significant!*

## SIGNIFICANT APPLICATION
‖‖‖‖‖‖‖‖‖‖‖‖‖‖‖‖‖‖‖‖‖‖‖‖‖‖‖‖‖‖‖‖‖‖‖‖‖‖‖‖‖‖‖‖‖‖‖‖‖‖‖‖‖‖‖‖‖‖‖‖‖‖‖‖‖‖‖‖‖‖‖‖‖‖‖‖‖

*1.* *What are some of the areas that make you feel small or make you want to hide rather than shine?*

_____

_____

_____

_____

*2.* *What are some areas that you need to re-position to prepare yourself for what God is wanting to do in you?*

_____

_____

_____

_____

*3.* *Do you have a "plan b"—something waiting for you in case this walk with Jesus doesn't work out? In other words, do you have something to fall back on if the calling of God you feel and heard doesn't pan out?*

_____

_____

_____

_____

4. Name one or two of the major moments you have had encountering God in your life.

_____

_____

_____

_____

5. How can you take that moment and make it a movement that helps you fulfill God's assignment on your life?

_____

_____

_____

_____